THE NATURAL HITTER'S

Drill Handbook

Vol. 3

101

DRILLS TO IMPROVE HITTING STRENGTH

Luis Ortiz

COACHES CHOICE™

ISBN: 978-1-60679-084-7
Library of Congress Control Number: 2009943799
Cover design: Studio J Art & Design and Brenden Murphy
Book layout: Bean Creek Studio
Front cover photo: ©Margaret Bowles/Cal Sport Media/ZUMA Press

Coaches Choice
P.O. Box 1828
Monterey, CA 93942
www.coacheschoice.com

Dedication

I want to dedicate this book:

- To my daughters, Gabriela, Naomi, Samantha (Boo-boo), and Moriah (Bebe), and my wife, Susan, for their patience and love.
- To my mother, Isabel, my dad, Luis, my brother, Yiyo, and my sisters, Tania and Ana, for their love, support, and encouragement in all the endeavors of my life.
- To all those kids that I have worked with through the winters who unknowingly tested many of these drills and provided the information I needed to write this book.

Acknowledgments

First, I would like to thank God for His love and mercy.

I also would like to thank Jay Gonzales and Brandon Kolb
for their help with the photos.

And I want to thank all of my friends (coaches and players) that provided insight
with the drills they have used to become better hitters.

Preface

My personal philosophy is that kids learn faster and better when they are having fun. The hitting lessons I teach and the instructional camps I help conduct are full of information, but that information is usually intertwined with analogies and drills that make hitting fun.

Even though I was not aware of the value of incorporating fun into my teaching efforts at the time, I started writing this book a long time ago. During my baseball journey, I have been blessed with playing in different countries and with players from all over the world. Since as long as I can remember, I have been writing down every hitting drill that I have seen or heard about, from the sophisticated drills used in Japan to the "take-advantage-of-everything approach" employed in the Dominican Republic and Cuba. I would always ask my friends what drills they usually did to get better. I then started creating drills for my own personal use or to help a teammate or client. I started writing this book all the way back in the mid-90s, when I was struggling a lot with injuries and wanted to prepare myself for life after baseball. I cannot believe how many drills I have gathered—so many, in fact, that I had to divide them into multiple volumes. I hope that you can find a number of drills in these volumes that help your players become the best hitters they can be. Have them follow the instructions for each drill, but do not be afraid of improvising for each player's personal hitting needs. All you can ask your hitters to do is to work hard, have fun, and persevere. Talk to each player, and have him watch himself on video to diagnose whatever problems he may be experiencing and then identify drills that target them. Look for drills that are appropriate for each individual, taking into consideration the equipment available, the weather, if he will be doing them alone or with a partner, and any other circumstances that are unique to that particular player.

Contents

1

Overview

Power Versus Hitting Power

Power is being able to apply maximum force in the shortest amount of time. In hitting, the more power a player generates during the swing, the harder he will hit the ball. But how can players develop more power and especially hitting power? Players have to get both stronger and faster to become more powerful. In this book, you will find drills that will help your players become stronger in a way that is systematic for hitting a baseball.

Hitting the ball hard is something that all hitters want to do. Being a powerful hitter with the ability to hit the ball out of the park is a goal most hitters have. While not everybody can be a home-run hitter, everybody can hit the ball hard. Hitting power is tricky because power is the combined application of strength and speed done in the least amount of time possible and at the proper moment—not the product of huge muscles. Thus, a weaker-looking hitter with a lot of bat speed and good timing will hit the ball harder and more consistently than a bigger guy with a slow bat.

Players can become more powerful by doing overload, overspeed, and rotational drills, which they should combine with a core area program and explosive exercises, thus stressing the muscles that are used for hitting. The premise of this book is that God made things simple: if people want to get faster, they do things fast; if they want to get stronger, they should use heavier weight. The greatest gift God has given people is the ability to adapt. If a hitter forces his body to do something that goes past his quitting point, he will improve. This book provides drills that will force your players to overload their hitting muscles, strengthening the muscles in a way that is going to help them hit the ball harder. They can do that by using a heavier bat and equipment, and swinging with high intensity (low reps and as explosively as possible). To develop bat speed, hitters need to challenge themselves to do something that they might think they are not capable of doing.

To hit the ball hard, hitters need strong muscles, not big ones. Players should develop stronger arms and shoulders, but they need to pay special attention to their core area or midsection (i.e., abs muscles, lower back, hips, and buttocks) as well as to their legs. Besides doing the drills in this book, your hitters should also follow a whole-body program that strengthens while still enabling them to have good range of motion through every joint, especially in the hips (for rotational purpose). The key word is *strength*, not size. Size does not mean that a hitter has gotten much stronger, because size comes from volume (high number of reps and sets) and the more reps or sets performed, the less weight a person can lift.

Many people still believe that hitting power comes from the wrists and forearms, but the truth is that most of the hitting power comes from the powerful momentum created by the violent rotation of the legs, hips, abs, and lower back (core area). That force is then transferred to the hands and wrists and then to the bat, which is why when a hitter performs a good swing, it looks like he is just using his arms. If you do not believe so, have one of your players sit on a stool at home plate and try to hit the ball out of the park.

To hit the ball hard, the whole body needs to work in unison to create bat speed and power. Your players need to pay attention to every muscle of the body, strengthening the body as a whole. A weaker part of the body will produce extra tension, and, as a result, extra energy and effort will be needed to produce bat speed.

To become powerful hitters, players need to work on the five components of conditioning—strength, power, endurance, flexibility, and speed—in a way that can be transferred to their swing. If they improve these components, they will perform better with less effort. The better-conditioned and more powerful your players are, the better the chance of being successful. Hitters will need to do resistance training to get stronger, explosive exercises to increase their power, overspeed training to improve their bat speed, a higher volume of repetitions to improve their hitting endurance (to be strong for the whole season and perform at the same level of intensity from the first inning to the last one), and stretching exercises to improve their flexibility and grace (especially in the hip area so they can rotate easily and powerfully). Your players should also combine all of these elements with a nutritious diet and the proper amount of rest to maximize results. In this book, you will find a lot of drills and exercises that will help improve the strength part of hitting. Use *The Natural Hitter's Drill Handbook Vol. 1: 101 Basic Hitting Drills* and *Vol. 2: 101 Advanced Hitting Drills* to complement your hitting program.

The Six Basic Drills

Before players begin utilizing hitting drills to improve their technique, you must teach them the six basic drills: dry swings, tee work, soft toss, flips, batting practice, and batting machine. These basics are the foundation for every drill included in this book, so it is essential that your players master them before moving on to more difficult drills.

One goal of this book was to keep things simple by using tips and pictures to help along the way. The following are terms used to keep things clear within each drill:

- Objectives—how the drill can help improve hitting technique
- Degree of Difficulty

    1B: Easy

    2B: Medium

    3B: Difficult

    HR: Extremely difficult

    GS: Most difficult
- Equipment Needed
- Description—step-by-step information on how to perform the drill
- Coaching Points—additional information, reminders, and safety guidelines to help your players get the most benefit from the drill

Dry Swings

A dry swing—a 1B-level tool—is a swing taken when there is not a ball involved. In other words, all you need for drills involving dry swings is a bat and some open space. Despite the simplicity, dry swings can be effective in teaching hitting mechanics, warming up for practice or games, and improving bat speed (when performed with different bat sizes).

Dry swings

To develop proper hitting mechanics, the hitter dry swings as follows:

- Stride: The front foot should be soft on the landing and point to home plate. The hands are taken back.
- The hitter takes his chin shoulder to shoulder during the swing.
- The back foot is pivoted as if squishing a bug with the big toe.
- The hitter keeps his head down, eyes on contact (visualize).
- Nice, short, and quick swing full of balance. The hitter swings, visualizing taking the bat head directly to the ball.
- For improving bat speed, the hitter swings his bat as fast as he can until he is fatigued.

Because dry swings do not feature a ball, the hitter can concentrate on his mechanics. He does not need to rush the swing as if a ball is involved.

Tee Work

Tee work can be used to correct and master hitting mechanics and as a way to discipline a hitter to stay back better so he can keep his power on his backside and improve his balance. Tee work will also help the hitter develop proper muscle memory. Tee work—a 2B-level tool—allows a hitter to focus on proper hitting mechanics and make adjustments. The equipment

Tee work

Soft tosses

needed in tee work drills is a tee, baseballs, a bat, and a batting cage or hitting net.

To perform these drills, the hitter needs to take his stride, land in his launching position, and "freeze." The hitter then swings the bat, aiming to hit the inside of the ball, or the seam closer to him (the ball should be set on the tee so the seams run perpendicular to the ground). During the swing, the hitter needs to go right to the ball, keeping his arms close to the body and letting the hands work first instead of the legs (the back knee follows the hands).

As a coach, it is important to emphasize a strong launching position and a proper hitting box, with the elbows pointing down, the front leg firm, the back knee flexed, and the back foot planted on the ground. The strength of this position dictates how the hitter hits the ball.

Soft Tosses

Soft tosses—another 2B-level tool—allow a hitter to take a lot of swings at a moving target without getting too tired, while also improving mechanics and bat speed. Soft tosses require a partner (or a "feeder") to toss the pitches, in addition to baseballs, a bat, a batting cage, and possibly a screen to protect the feeder.

To perform soft tosses, the hitter takes his normal stance at home plate as a partner positions himself on

the other side of the plate in a 45-degree angle to the hitter. The partner is either on one of his knees or sits on a chair. The distance between hitter and feeder is about eight to 10 feet, a distance at which the feeder will not get hit by the bat. When the hitter and the feeder are in the right position, the feeder then softly tosses the ball underhand to the hitter. The hitter waits back and hits the ball right to the middle of the net. The hitter will have to experiment with where he wants the ball to be tossed and occasionally may want to vary the location of the toss.

This drill is one of the best available for developing sound mechanics and improving bat speed, and is performed almost every day by professional players before practices and games.

Flips

Flips are similar to soft tosses in that they improve a hitter's mechanics while saving the thrower's arm. A 2B-level tool, flips require a bat, baseballs, a batting cage or field, a screen, and maybe a chair. The hitter should do this drill often. Most professional hitters take flips before every batting practice.

The person flipping the balls gets behind the screen about 15 to 20 feet in front of the hitter, in the direction where a pitcher would set up. The "flipper" tosses the ball underhand in a softball motion. He tosses the ball over the plate as the hitter aims to hit the screen every

Flips

Batting practice

time, always focusing on good mechanics. Remind the flipper to make sure he brings his arm behind the screen quickly after releasing the ball to avoid being hit. It is easier for the flipper to do this when standing up, but it can be done sitting down as well.

Timing is of the essence in this drill. The hitter starts the swing process (striding) when the flipper is taking his arm back. The hitter should be landing the front foot just as the flipper is letting go of the ball to ensure a separation of the stride and hands.

Batting Practice

Batting practice mimics game conditions, thereby improving the hitter's timing and preparing him for game speed. This drill allows the hitter to see how hard and to where he is hitting the ball. Batting practice—a 2B-level tool—requires baseballs, a bat, helmet, partner, and either a batting cage or a field and "L" screen.

The hitter sets up at home plate with the partner about two-thirds of the way to the pitcher's mound. The partner then tosses the ball by mimicking a pitcher's windup and throwing fastballs straight and firm (though not too hard). At the hitter's request the partner can throw off-speed pitches. Batting practices are usually done in groups of three to five hitters, and usually with five rounds per group.

Every hitter needs to use batting practice to get better and get ready for the game, not as a home run hitting contest. The hitter should practice his game plan and prepare to do what he might do in the game.

Professional baseball teams often follow a batting practice routine that goes something like this:

Round 1: Two bunts, one hit and run, one move the runner, five hits to the opposite field

Round 2: One infield in, one infield back, five hits, one squeeze bunt

Round 3: Five hits (hit it where it is pitched)

Round 4: Three hits (driving the ball)

Round 5: Base hit rounds (if the hitter gets a hit, he keeps hitting; if he gets an out, the next hitter hits). If there is time, another base hit round is done.

Batting Machine

Batting machine practice drills allow hitters to practice their swings often and to see different speeds during the drill. A 2B-level tool, batting machine drills require a bat, baseballs, a batting machine, and a batting cage.

A hitter swinging off a batting machine needs to move around home plate to simulate inside, outside, low, high, hard, and slow pitches. The hitter should always wear a helmet to protect himself.

Batting machine

To develop a great swing, a combination of these types of drills should be performed every day. For example, professional hitters, the best in the business, do underhand flips, tee work, and batting practice before nearly every game. They might do them with their own personal touch to target a problem or a feel, but they consistently do these drills because they know that they keep them sharp or help them get out of slumps when they are struggling.

Every player needs to develop his own program, with drills that keep his swing consistent and razor-sharp. When setting up this program, the coach can combine two or three drills of different types to accelerate a player's improvement. For example, perform soft toss hitting colored balls with a heavy bat. Soft toss helps improve hitting mechanics, while colored balls improve how well a hitter sees the ball. And with the heavy bat, the player will be overloading his hitting muscles and getting stronger. You will save time by having each player perform hard, smart work.

Off-season vs. In-season

During the off-season, each player should perform drills that make him stronger, help him swing faster, and make his swing mechanically sound. Off-season drill work is especially important for players whose regular seasons involve a lot of games each week. Players who only play one or two games a week can continue doing the same drills that they were doing during the off-season, but should avoid overload and/or overspeed drills before a game. Mechanics drills can and should be done every single day of the season, but be sure to work on quality over quantity.

Players who play four to seven days a week should perform in-season drills that reinforce what they did during the off-season and back off of the overload/overspeed drills so they do not fatigue during the game or run out of gas during the second half of the season. This guideline does not apply to backup players who are not playing much. These hitters should take advantage of their time, push themselves, and make themselves better by working harder so they can eventually become regulars.

Remember, every player is different. Some hitters love to work hard every day and it does not seem to affect their game, while others cannot do it. Learn about each player. Have them make mental notes of how they feel during games after different levels of intensity during practice and then find a level that keeps them energized during the whole game. Also, remind your team that getting good sleep and having a nutritious diet will also help them stay stronger longer.

Every player must work hard to find the routine that works best for him. Once it is found, help the player to be consistent with it so he stays in top condition during the whole year. It is better to do a little work every day than a lot once in a while.

Proper Drill Workout Sequence

Players should use the following sequence when doing drills:
- Warm-up
- Bat speed, power, and reaction drills
- Mechanics and mental drills (improve skills)
- Balance, hand-eye coordination, and vision drills
- Team and game situation drills
- Overload drills
- Conditioning drills
- Cool-down

For example, if on Monday the team is doing bat speed and vision drills the sequence should be warm-up, bat speed drills, vision drills, and cool-down. Bat speed, power, and reaction drills should be done first because players should be as fresh as possible when trying to improve power and bat speed. Conditioning drills come last because the goal is to improve work capacity and will power (the ability to keep going when wanting to quit) and these are best improved when players are already tired.

The following guidelines will help the team get the most out of drills. Distribute this list to every player.

- Concentrate and think about what you are doing. A drill is supposed to feel mechanical at first, but the more you do it, the more natural it will become.
- Do drills game speed. Do not simply go through the motions. You need to mimic game conditions even if you are doing tee work or dry swinging. Do the drills in the manner you want to perform during the game. You might feel slow at the beginning, but always perform drills with intensity.
- Be safe. Before doing a drill, look around so you do not hit anybody. Tell people what you are doing if they are on the field. Use tennis shoes in the cage or on a carpet. Do not overstrain yourself. If it hurts, stop. Use batting gloves to prevent blisters whenever you are taking a lot of swings.
- Do not overdo it. Stop when you are getting tired or when the intensity level is decreasing. When you are tired, you will either begin using the very habit you are working to break or help yourself with other parts of the body, thereby creating additional problems.
- With drills that require a partner, make sure that the feeder knows what he is doing and what you are trying to accomplish. He needs to be accurate and be able to point out when you are doing something right or wrong. He needs to make sure that he stays behind the screen at all times.
- Grow into each drill. If you are a beginner, stick with the beginner's drills and move up as you get better and stronger. Do not get ahead of yourself.

It is more beneficial to do something right at an easier level than to be inconsistent at a more difficult one.

- Do what the drill tells you to do, but do not be afraid to change it to your advantage. It is your drill now, so target your personal need even if that requires adjusting the drill.
- Ask your coach what you need to work on, and then find a drill that targets your needs.
- Always do a set of regular swings after doing the drill so you can transfer the feeling of the drill to your swing.
- To improve bat speed and power swing faster than you normally do. Challenge yourself to do more than you think possible.
- The keys of success are:
    ✓ Be intense—work hard, pay the price.
    ✓ Be persistent—work often, be patient (the race is not always won by the strongest or fastest, but by the one that lasts the longest). Remember, the key of succeeding with a drill is repetition.
    ✓ Be smart—work with a plan, do what works for you.
    ✓ Enjoy what you are doing.

Begin the drill-selection process by looking at what problem a drill targets, what skill level it requires, and whether you have the equipment to do it in practice. After you have checked the drills and found the ones that target a particular player's problem, be persistent and have the player perform the drill often. Repetition is the key for any muscle memory practice. Remember, you are helping the players to get rid of something (i.e., a bad habit) they have been doing for a while, so give them the time needed to eliminate the problem and succeed. Remind the players that they need to repeat a good habit for a few weeks if they want to get rid of an old bad habit. They must be patient, work hard, and be smart. If they do that they will conquer any hitting problem they might have and become the hitters they believe they can be.

2

Drills That Overload the Hitting Muscles Using Weighted Equipment

Drill #1: Swinging Wearing a Weighted Vest

Objectives:
- Develops power (overload)
- Develops bat speed (overspeed)
- Develops hip flexibility
- Improves use of the legs during the swing
- Develops explosiveness on lazy hips and leg pivot
- Strengthens the core area and the hitting muscles

Degree of Difficulty:
- Dry swings: 2B
- Tee work: 2B
- Soft tosses: 3B
- Flips: 3B
- Batting practice: 4B

Equipment Needed:
- Bat
- Baseballs
- Batting cage, hitting net, baseball field, or open space
- Weighted vest
- Optional: Tee

Description: This drill is simple to learn, but strenuous to do. The hitter simply puts the vest on and starts swinging. It is as simple as that. The hitter should not use a weight heavier than 10 percent of his body weight. Younger hitters especially should stay within around 5 percent of their weight. The hitter should follow the 10-plus-5 routine, where he swings 10 times with the vest on and five times with the vest off. Stronger hitters can take the back knee straight down, not only to strengthen the legs but to see how well the weight is distributed between the legs. If the hitter is lunging or falling back, he will not be able to go straight down.

Coaching Points:
- The hitter should not use a vest so heavy that he cannot move. The idea is to get a vest that is heavy enough to offer him good resistance and light enough that it will allow him to swing explosively to develop power. Remember the essence of power is speed. The hitter should concentrate on doing each swing faster than the prior one.
- The hitter should warm up extensively and do this drill as a complement to his strengthening program.
- Three to four sets (10-plus-5) of this drill should be performed every other day, especially during the off-season, but never before a game.
- As with any strengthening program, the hitter should allow adequate rest and recovery time between workouts to replenish his energy and to let the muscle heal.
- Weighted vests can be purchased in many sporting goods stores or ordered from companies that sell track and field equipment.
- Complement this drill with a core area (abs, lower back, hips, buttocks) strengthening program.

Drill #2: Wrist Weight

Objectives:
- Develops power (overload)
- Develops bat speed (overspeed)
- Develops hands-to-the-ball feeling

Degree of Difficulty:
- Dry swings: 2B
- Tee work: 2B
- Soft tosses: 3B
- Flips: HR

Equipment Needed:
- A pair of wrist or ankle weights (1 to 5 pounds)
- Bat and balls
- Batting cage or net

Description: This drill is another overload (heavier than usual) and overspeed (faster than usual) drill. The hitter wraps the weights around his wrists, and then he takes his natural swing. After he starts his swing, he will notice how the hands just go. This drill can be done with soft tosses, flips, tee work, or dry swings. When the hitter swings with the weights on, the swing will be slower. For that reason, he has to complete this drill by taking a few swings without the weights.

Coaching Points:
- The hitter should do a couple of sets of 10 reps with the weights on, followed by five swings without the weights. The hitter should experience that extra bat speed, because to increase bat speed, the hitter needs to swing faster than usual.
- A good idea is to progress from a lighter weight to a heavier weight.
- The hitter should warm up properly and make sure to rest between practice sessions.

Drill #3: Weighted Gloves Overload

Objective: Develops hitting strength

Degree of Difficulty:
- Dry swings: 2B
- Tee work: 2B
- Soft tosses: 3B
- Flips: 3B
- Batting practice: HR

Equipment Needed:
- A pair of weighted gloves (1 to 2 pounds)
- Bat and balls
- Batting cage or net

Description: This drill is another overload (heavier-than-usual) drill. The difference between this drill and Drill #2 is that with the wrist weights the hitter will feel the resistance obviously on the wrist, and with this drill he will feel it more on his hands. The hitter wears the gloves as normal, and then he takes his natural swing. After he starts his swing, he will notice how the hands just go. This drill can be done with soft tosses, flips, tee work, or dry swings. When the hitter swings with the weights on, the swing will be slower. Therefore, he has to complete this drill by taking a few swings without them.

Coaching Points:
- Weighted gloves can be bought at many sporting goods stores; weighted batting gloves can be bought online.
- The hitter should do a couple of sets of 10 reps with the weights on, followed by five swings without them.
- A good idea is to progress from a lighter weight to a heavier weight.
- The hitter should warm up properly and make sure to rest between practice sessions.

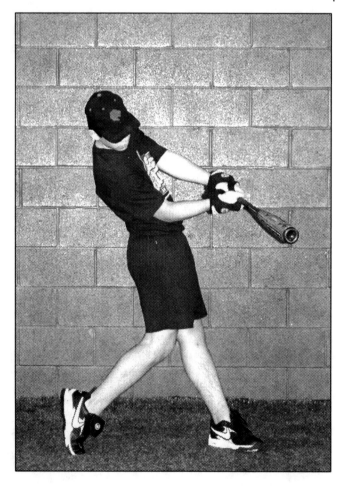

Drill #4: Sled Pull

Objectives:
- Improves rotation and hitting strength
- Improves balance and body coordination

Degree of Difficulty: 2B+ (depending on weight used)

Equipment Needed:
- A weight plate or tire
- A rope or dog leash
- Open space
- Optional: Partner and another tire

Description: The hitter ties a rope or loops a dog leash or something similar through the hole of the weight or tire. The weight or tire is pulled on the ground. Depending on the space available, he can do one of three things:
- In slow motion, the hitter pulls the weight in front of the toes, turning the back leg and pulling the hand at the same time. The hitter wants a complete pivot of the back leg, and the gradual snapping of the front knee. The hitter keeps taking the hands (especially the top hand) forward, going through the full swing motion (pushing the hands away). The hitter or partner pulls the weight back to the starting position and repeats.
- If the space is big, the hitter can pull the weight or tire forward, and then walk a couple steps away from the weight until the rope is straight again. The hitter then repeats.
- If the hitter has a partner and two ropes, the hitter can set himself to the other side of the partner. As the hitter pulls the weight away, the partner's rope will get extended, and he performs the drill going in the opposite direction of the hitter.

Coaching Points:
- The weight of the plate will depend on the hitter.
- To mimic his swing, the hitter can use a bat.

Drill #5: Slow Bat Swing With Sled

Objective: Improves hitting strength by overloading the hitting muscles

Degree of Difficulty: 2B to HR (depending on weight used)

Equipment Needed:
- Bat
- Rope and weight
- Batting cage

Description: The hitter prepares the sled by tying one end of a rope to a 5- or 10-pound weight plate (depending on the hitter's strength) and the other end to the bat head (taped for safety). The hitter places the weight on the ground in the direction of the catcher and positions himself at his launching position, but the hands are lower. The hitter then pulls the weight forward, turning the back foot and pulling the hands forward at the same time while keeping the front leg strong. The hitter keeps going and finishes his swing by dragging the weight forward as far as possible. For convenience, the hitter simply walks forward, ties the rope, and repeats. The hitter does 10 reps, takes a break, and repeats the drill.

Coaching Points:
- The hitter needs to make sure that the weight is not so heavy that he will not be able to drag it.
- This drill is better done in a batting cage.

Drill #6: Wrist Torque With Sled

Objective: Improves hitting strength by overloading the hitting muscles

Degree of Difficulty: 2B to HR (depending on weight used)

Equipment Needed:
- Bat
- Rope and weight
- Batting cage

Description: The hitter prepares the sled by tying one end of a rope to a 5- or 10-pound weight plate (depending on the hitter's strength) and the other end to the bat head (taped for safety). The hitter places the weight on the ground in the direction of the catcher and positions himself in his contact position (hands in front of bat, bat head in an angle back to the catcher, eyes on the ball, back knee pointing to the ball, and back foot on big toe). The hitter then uses his hands to create wrist torque on contact by pulling the bottom hand back to the front shoulder and pushing the top hand forward toward the pitcher.

The hitter drags the weight forward. For convenience, the hitter simply walks forward, ties the rope and repeats. The hitter does 10 reps, and then takes a break (he can also reverse the action, as if he were switching hitting to strengthen both arms to hit the ball hard).

Coaching Point: The hitter needs to make sure that the weight is not so heavy that he will not be able to drag it.

Drill #7: Wrist Weight With Hold

Objectives:
- Improves arm strength
- Teaches the hitter to be more efficient during the swing
- Improves balance and core stability

Degree of Difficulty:
- Dry swings: 2B
- Tee work: 2B
- Soft tosses: 3B
- Flips: 3B

Equipment Needed:
- Wrist weights or gloves
- Bat and baseballs
- Batting cage

Description: The hitter can do this drill during dry swings and tee work if working by himself and/or soft toss and flips when working with a partner. The hitter places a pair of heavy gloves or wrist weights around his wrists, with the weight used depending on the hitter's age and strength level. The hitter takes his stride and his hands back. He then holds his hands back for five seconds. The partner tosses the ball, and the hitter swings, trying to have a swing in which the weights feel light. The heavier the weight feels, the farther the hands go from the body (casting or dropping them). When the weight feels light, the hitter has found his optimal launching position and beginning of his swing approach.

Coaching Points:
- The weight used should be determined by the hitter's strength, not going past five pounds.
- Younger hitters can make their own wrist weights by using a pair of sanitary socks (baseball socks) and filling them with sand. Young hitters should start with half a pound per sock and can increase the weight as they grow older and stronger.

Drill #8: Ankle Weight on Handle

Objective: Improves torque on contact

Degree of Difficulty:
- Dry swings: 2B
- Soft tosses: 3B

Equipment Needed:
- A bat
- Ankle weight or doughnut
- Open space

Description: The hitter wraps an ankle weight or places a doughnut on the bat so it is touching the top of his top hand during the grip. The ankle weight should be tight enough that the weight will not fly off the bat during the swing. This overloading drill will work the hitting muscles and force the hitter to extend his arms powerfully through the ball. This drill can be done during dry swings the following ways:
- The hitter swings the bat and stops when he forms the power V on extension.
- The hitter can do his normal swing, finishing on his follow-through.

The drill can also be done with a regular soft toss, with the hitter trying to hit the ball with the ankle weight.

Coaching Points:
- The weight should start low and progress to a higher weight as the hitter starts getting stronger.
- The hitter needs to warm up properly before doing this drill. The wrists and the shoulders are working to the max during this drill, and should be warmed up accordingly to avoid injury.

Drill #9: Ankle Weight on Handle, Flying off Bat

Objective: Improves torque on contact

Degree of Difficulty: 3B

Equipment Needed:
- Bat
- Ankle weight or doughnut
- Open space

Description: The hitter ties an ankle weight so it is touching the top of his top hand during the grip. The ankle weight should be loose enough that the weight could easily fly off the bat during the swing. This overloading drill will work the hitting muscles and force the hitter to extend his arms powerfully through the ball. This drill should only be done during dry swings. The hitter should perform his normal swing and finish on his follow-through.

Coaching Points:
- The weight of the ankle weight should start low and progress to a higher weight as the hitter starts getting stronger.
- The hitter needs to warm up properly before doing this drill. The wrists and the shoulders are working to the max during this drill, and should be warmed up accordingly to avoid injury.

Drill #10: Weight on the Knob of the Bat

Objectives:
- Develops power (overload)
- Develops bat speed (overspeed)
- Helps the hitter to swing down

Degree of Difficulty:
- Dry swings: 2B
- Tee work: 2B
- Soft tosses: 3B
- Flips: 3B
- Batting practice: HR

Equipment Needed:
- A bat
- Baseballs
- Batting cage, hitting net, base field or open space
- A tee (optional)
- A ProCut® or a small weight/tape

Description: To do this drill, a weighted object is attached at the knob (end of the handle) of the bat. This placement changes the balance of the bat, making it heavier at the hands. This drill allows the hitter to swing down easier, plus overloading the hands with the extra weight and strengthening them. The weight on the knob makes the bat feel the opposite as when using a doughnut. With the doughnut, the hitter might tend to throw the head of the bat to the ball first, making him go around the ball. By having the weight on the knob, the hitter will always throw the hands first, and the head just follows. A hitter can use a couple objects for this drill:
- A product named ProCut is sold in baseball catalogs. A lot of Major Leaguers use them. They are easily attached to the bat, and they are designed with different weights. Many professional players use them during practice.
- A player can make his own version by taping a removable end of a light dumbbell used for aerobic exercise to the end of a batting practice bat. He needs to make sure it is not too heavy, though (8 to 16 ounces should be good).
- A light ankle weight can also be used for this purpose.

Coaching Points:
- The hands just go when the weight is taken of the bat. The hitter needs to always take a few swings without the weight after every 10 swings with the weight on the bat.
- The hitter needs to make sure he is swinging down, throwing the hands first, and then the rest of the bat.
- This drill can be used as a warm-up before practices or games.

Drill #11: Slow-Motion Swing

Objectives:
- Improves arm strength
- Improves balance

Degree of Difficulty: 2B+ (depending on weight used)

Equipment Needed:
- Small or regular bat
- Doughnut, ankle weight, or heavy bat

Description: The slow-motion swing is another overload drill that not only will help the hitter get stronger, but also become more efficient during the swing process. The hitter does a slow-motion swing with a weighted bat (weight on barrel). The hitter needs to go from beginning to end as slow as he can (trying to go about an inch per second). After each set, the hitter can do a set of his regular swing with his regular bat as fast as he can, with or without a ball being involved. The way this drill helps the hitter become more efficient is a result of how hard gravity pulls down on the bat. If the hitter's hands get away from him, the bat will seem heavy and harder to swing in slow motion. If the hitter keeps the hands close to the body until contact and then extends through the ball to the power V, the weight will feel easier to manage.

Coaching Points:
- To make this drill more challenging, the hitter can hold at arm extension for a count of one or two. He can also come back in slow motion to increase the degree of difficulty.
- The weight of the bat will depend on the strength of the hitter. This drill requires body control, so the hitter should use a lighter weight but do the drill correctly, rather than using a heavier weight but not have any balance or perform in a sloppy manner.
- This drill will not only work on arm strength, but also on balance and body coordination.

Drill #12: Ankle-Weight-on-Back-Foot Pivot

Objectives:
- Teaches the hitter to pivot properly
- Increases power by pushing the hitter to overload the back leg during the drill

Degree of Difficulty:
- Dry swings: 1B
- Tee work: 1B
- Soft tosses: 2B
- Flips: 2B
- Batting practice/machine: 3B

Equipment Needed:
- The heaviest ankle weight available
- Bat and balls

Description: For this drill, the hitter puts an ankle weight on the back foot. This drill will help the hitter accomplish two different things:

- During the stride, the ankle weight will force the foot to keep the heel down, avoiding any leaking of power.
- During the pivot, the ankle weight will both teach the hitter how to pivot properly because the weight will make the hitter feel what the foot is doing, and it will strengthen the back leg so the hitter could pivot more powerfully when he does it without the weight.

Coaching Points:
- The ankle weight should be placed on the foot so its heaviest part is on the outside of the shoe.
- The hitter needs to make sure to pivot the foot by driving through the ball. It should feel as if the back knee and hip are pulling the foot. At the end of the swing, the back knee should be near the front knee, and the tip of the back foot should be touching the ground, with the heel pointing to the sky.

Drill #13: Four-Ankle-Weight Power Swings

Objectives:
- Strengthens hitting muscles
- Slows the body to help the hitter see the ball better
- Slows the hitter to allow the coach to see any bad habit that he cannot see at regular speed

Degree of Difficulty:
- Dry swings: 1B
- Tee work: 1B
- Soft tosses: 2B
- Flips: 2B

Equipment Needed:
- Four ankle weights (1 to 5 pounds for hands; 5 pounds or more for legs)
- A bat
- Baseballs
- Optional: Partner, tee

Description: For this drill, the hitter needs four ankle weights. He ties two weights around his ankles and two around his wrists, and then tries to swing the bat as he normally does. The ankle weight will force him to keep the feet in place, giving him instant feedback on how and where he should be moving his feet. The wrist weight will overload the hitting muscles of the arms and core. This drill saves time by working on different skills at the same time.

Coaching Points:
The hitter needs to make sure to warm up properly before doing this drill. This drill will improve:
- Back leg pivot
- Softness of the front foot on the approach
- Strength of the arms and legs
- Casting (if the hitter takes his hands away from the body, gravity will pull the weight down and make him work harder). If the swing seems easy, the hitter has found his true power position.

Drill #14: Holding at Different Positions With a Weighted Vest

Objectives:
- Improves balance
- Improves leg strength
- Develops muscle memory

Degree of Difficulty: 2B

Equipment Needed:
- Adjustable weighted vest
- Bat
- Clock or partner with stopwatch

Description: The hitter first sets the weight of the weighted vest to 10 percent of how much he weighs (better conditioned athletes can try a higher percentage, but this should be the starting point). If the hitter weighs 150 pounds, the weight on the weighted vest should be 15 pounds. The hitter then holds for 30 seconds at the following three positions:
- Launching position (after taking a step)—Note: This position is the most important one to work in this drill. After landing his stride, the hitter should

look as if he is one-quarter of the way to finishing a squat.
- Contact area
- Follow-through

After he can master the 30 seconds, he can do one of two things:
- Increase the time to 45 seconds (eventually to 60 seconds)
- Keep the time the same, but increase the weight by one or two pounds

Coaching Points:
- Younger hitters do not need to use the vest. Just holding is a workout for them. When young hitters are ready to use the vest, coaches should be cautious and listen to them when they say the weight is too heavy.
- The hitter can do a couple of sets of this drill, especially during the off-season to get stronger and to enhance balance for the upcoming season.

Drill #15: Front Arm

Objective: Strengthens the lead arm for the swing

Degree of Difficulty: 3B

Equipment Needed:
• Dumbbell (2 to 10 pounds)
• Cable pulley machine
• Optional: Bat

Description: This drill can be done with either a dumbbell or a cable. For the dumbbell, the hitter lies down on his back-arm side on a regular weight bench. Holding a dumbbell on his front hand with the arm extended and almost touching the ground, the hitter brings the weight up by extending at the elbow. He should use a weight between 2 and 10 pounds, depending on his level of strength.

With a cable pulley, the hitter stands perpendicular to the machine with the grip handle about chest high. With the arm flexed, the hitter brings the arm straight out in front of his body without moving the body, or turns the body, mimicking the swing. The hitter can use more weight with the cable pulley than with the dumbbell.

The hitter repeats the exercise for the desired number of reps. After each set, he takes five swings with his bat if possible.

Coaching Points:
• The hitter needs to make sure that the weight is not so heavy that he is going to hurt himself. It is better to use a lighter weight with good form than a heavier weight with poor mechanics.
• The reps should be done with full range of motion, after the hitter has warmed up properly.

Drill #16: Dumbbell Strength and Arm Extension

Objectives:
- Strengthens the arms for hitting
- Improves arm extension

Degree of Difficulty: 1B

Equipment Needed:
- Dumbbells of different weights, starting at five pounds
- An open space (batting cage or gym)

Description: The hitter does this drill starting with a five-pound dumbbell, and then increases the weight as he gets stronger and more comfortable. The hitter starts with the front arm. He grabs the dumbbell as he normally grips his bat with the bottom hand. He then brings the arm close to the body with the fingers on the weight touching or right over the back shoulder. The hitter brings the weight forward (bottom end of the dumbbell) slowly over the outside of the front hip, only extending the elbow (he does not take the arm forward to the pitcher). The hitter does a set of 10 reps, and then does the back arm. For the back arm, the hitter grabs the weight as he normally grips his bat with the top hand. The hitter can do the back arm two ways. The hitter starts as his normal launching position. He brings the arm forward slowly right in front of the chest, keeping it flexed. When the arm cannot go forward anymore, he extends the arm, getting the weight over the front hip. Additionally, the hitter can start with the dumbbell already in front of the chest and just extend the arm forward (after the set is over, he should repeat with the other arm). The hitter can also use both hands at the same time. After a couple of sets, the hitter takes his bat and performs a few regular swings.

Coaching Points:
- This drill is for hitters 16 years and older. Younger hitters should get permission from their parents and be supervised if they do it.
- The hitter should never use dumbbells so heavy that he cannot do the mechanic correctly. It is better to use lighter weight and do it properly than to use heavier weight and, as a result, develop poor mechanics.
- The arm only extends to where contact will be made, and then flexes back.

3

Drills That Overload the Hitting Muscles Using Tires and Punching Bags

Drill #17: Hitting a Tire

Objectives:
- Improves power
- Improves bat speed
- Improves hitting strength

Degree of Difficulty: 2B

Equipment Needed:
- An old tire
- Rope
- A bat (preferably an old wood bat)

Description: A rope is tied around the tire (like a tire swing), and then hung in a tree or something similar. The tire should be around waist high, depending on what the hitter is working on (high, low pitches). The hitter hits the tire's tread. This method is the best because the hitter will be able to finish his swing; plus, the tire gives in after being hit, thus releasing tension and avoiding injury.

Note: This drill should never be performed with a static tire (i.e., with a tire nailed or stuck to something so it does not move after being hit) for the following reasons:

- The hitter cannot finish his swing, which will prevent him from working on the correct swinging mechanics.
- Because the tire cannot give in after being hit, the reaction of the hitting action will come back to the hitter, potentially causing injury.

Coaching Points:
- The hitter can draw a baseball (with white paint) on each side of the tire's tread (low on one side, high on the other). Doing so will incorporate eye-hand coordination to the drill.
- The hitter should engage in some kind of hitting practice right after each set. Doing so will develop bat speed.
- Just as in weight training, when the hitter hits a tire, he is overloading his hitting muscles. Proper rest is essential (two or three times per week with at least a day off in between).
- A good program could be three or four sets of 10 to 25 swings per section.
- To avoid injury, the hitter can tape his wrists or wear wristbands.

Drill #18: Angled Tire Swing

Objectives:
- Improves power and contact
- Improves the swing by leveling it for hitting better through the ball

Degree of Difficulty: 2B

Equipment Needed:
- A tire
- Two ropes
- High and sturdy place to hang the tire
- An old wood bat

Description: For this drill, the hitter is going to need a tire, two ropes, and a high and sturdy location from which to hang the tire. The hitter ties up the tire such that when the tire hangs, its hole is parallel to the ground (instead of perpendicular as it is typically set up). The rope closest to the hitter should always be shorter so the side of the tire that is farther from the hitter is lower than the side closest to him. The rope should be adjusted according to the height of the pitch being practiced, to make the angle of the tire simulate the pitch. The higher the pitch, the flatter the angle. The lower the pitch, the steeper the angle. The hitter then hits the tire, keeping his hands above the barrel of the bat, so the bat is also at an angle.

Coaching Point: The hitter should try Drill #17: Hitting a Tire before doing this drill.

Drill #19: Hitting the Inside of a Tire to Make It Spin

Objectives:
- Teaches the hitter to stay inside the ball
- Strengthens the hitter by overloading his hitting muscle

Degree of Difficulty: 2B

Equipment Needed:
- A tire and rope (hanging)
- An old wood bat

Description: The hitter hangs a medium to small size tire, resembling a tire swing. Instead of hitting the thread of the tire as the regular tire drill, the hitter can do this drill two different ways:
- Hit the outside of the front of the thread to make the tire rotate clockwise.
- Hit the inside of the tire where it connects to the wheel (inside hole) to make the tire rotate clockwise.

Coaching Point: The idea is to make the tire rotate as many times as possible.

Drill #20: Punching Bag Contact

Objectives:
- Improves contact strength
- Teaches hitter to hit through the ball

Degree of Difficulty: 2B

Equipment Needed:
- A bat
- A punching bag (between 10 and 50 pounds, depending on the hitter's strength)

Description: The hitter sets up in front of the punching bag in his regular stance. The hitter swings, remaining aware that the punching bag will give him a lot of resistance and that he is not going to finish his swing. He is basically stopping on his extension (power V, right after contact). The hitter needs to have a firm grip and strong leg position (back foot on big toe and front leg firm). He should do at least a couple sets of at least 10 repetitions.

Coaching Points:
- The hitter can find punching bags at any sporting goods store or department store.
- The hitter needs to make sure to use his legs and maintain proper mechanics when doing this drill.
- If possible, he should do any of the hitting practices after each set of this drill.

Drill #21: Punching Bag Extension

Objectives:
- Improves power
- Improves arm strength
- Improves arm extension

Degree of Difficulty: 2B

Equipment Needed:
- A punching bag
- Bat

Description: The hitter stands next to the punching bag with his bat, resembling the contact position (he can also hit the punching bag with a swing and stop on contact). The hitter pushes the punching bag away from him, doing some reps in slow motion and others at regular speed. To make the drill more difficult, the hitter sets the punching bag right in front of his chest. To work on the wrist and forearms, he places the punching bag farther away from him (with his arms extended). As part of this drill, the hitter can get next to the punching bag without his bat, holding the punching bag with his hands, and explosively toss it away from him in the direction of the pitcher. A variation of the punching bag toss is for the hitter to hold the punching bag with the forearm and upper part of his back arm and throw it away from him.

Coaching Point: The hitter can use an old wood bat for this drill.

Drill #22: Punching Bag and Tire

Objectives:
- Improves the mechanics of rotation
- Improves core strength and rotational power

Degree of Difficulty: 2B

Equipment Needed:
- A punching bag
- A tire
- Rope
- A wood bat or old metal bat

Description: The hitter hangs the punching bag on something high and sturdy. The tire is placed behind the back foot. The hitter starts the drill with the bat in a contact position with the punching bag (hands in front of the punching bag, bat head back at an angle). He then pushes the punching bag forward and the tire back simultaneously in slow motion.

A variation of this drill is to use a heavy bat and turn the tire on the floor in slow motion as the hitter mimics a slow-motion swing with the heavy bat. He keeps the hands inside the back, gets to the hanging punching bag, and pushes the tire as he is trying to finish the pivot of the back foot.

Coaching Points:
- The idea is to have the hitter push forward with the hands as the back foot is pushing back to create torque and a powerful rotation.
- The punching bag and tire size would depend on the hitter's strength. They should not be so heavy that the hitter cannot move them.
- After a few reps, the hitter can hit some regular balls with the tire behind the back foot. He should follow with a few swings without the tire.

Drill #23: One-Handed Swing at a Tire

Objective: Improves hitting strength by overloading the hitting muscles

Degree of Difficulty: 2B

Equipment Needed:
- Smaller or regular bat
- Old tire and rope
- High sturdy location to hang tire

Description: The hitter hangs a tire or punching bag to something high and sturdy. The hitter should use a bat considerably smaller than what he normally uses or really choke up on his regular bat (i.e., to almost below the barrel). The hitter takes his normal stance in front of the tire. The hitter then takes one of his hands off the bat, and places it either on his side or behind his back. After that, the hitter swings, hitting the tire as hard as he can and working on the proper mechanics of each arm.
- Bottom hand: The hitter does not force the wrist to roll over. The bottom hand starts the swing, so acceleration is a must. The hitter needs to keep the inside of his upper arm close to the chest.
- Top hand: The hitter swings down, and tries to hit the ball on a 45-degree angle. It is as if the hitter is trying to hit the ball with his palm.
- Rest of the body: The hitter does the same thing as if doing a regular swing, emphasizing keeping the head down and a firm front let.

Coaching Point: The hitter should do a set of regular one-arm swings after every set of the one-arm tire drill.

Drill #24: Strong Position Hold

Objective: Improves hitting strength by overloading the hitting muscles

Degree of Difficulty: 2B

Equipment Needed:
- Bat
- Tire, punching bag, plus strong rope
- Partner

Description: The hitter sets himself in his contact position. A partner then tosses a heavy hanging object (such as a punching bag, tire, ankle weight, or milk jug filled with sand) to the hitter. The hitter then tries to hold his strong position by not losing his balance or allowing the bat to give when the object hits the bat. The speed of the toss or heaviness of the object will depend on the hitter's age and strength.

Coaching Point: The hitter needs to make sure that the object used is not so heavy that could hurt him.

Drill #25: Tire and Punching Bag Three-Sound Swing

Objectives:
- Improves contact
- Makes the swing more compact
- Improves bat speed

Degree of Difficulty: 2B

Equipment Needed:
- One or two tires
- A punching bag
- A bat
- Baseballs
- Batting cage
- Optional: Partner, tee

Description: For this drill, the hitter will need a tire and a punching bag or two tires (or any similar object). The hitter stands in front of a hanging tire, and places a punching bag within his legs. The hitter then tries to swing by "hearing" the back knee hitting the punching bag, the bat hitting the tire, and the back shoulder hitting the bottom of the chin all at the same time. If one of these factors is off, then the hitter is not using maximum power on contact. This drill will not only maximize power but also synchronize the swing in a way that is more efficient and consistent.

Coaching Point: This great drill gives a hitter a purpose to swing the bat. By trying to "listen" to the three sounds, the hitter becomes more consistent and allows him to swing faster.

Drill #26: Holding a Punching Bag

Objectives:
- Improves power
- Improves arm strength
- Improves arm extension

Degree of Difficulty: 2B

Equipment Needed:
- A punching bag
- A bat

Description: The hitter stands next to the punching bag in his regular stance. The hitter hits the bag powerfully. He then pushes the bag away and holds a complete arm extension for a determined number of seconds (if he is doing reps) or for as long as he can.

Coaching Point: The hitter can use an old wood bat for this drill.

Drill #27: Rapid-Fire Punching Bag Swings

Objectives:
- Improves power
- Improves arm strength

Degree of Difficulty: 2B

Equipment Needed:
- A punching bag
- A bat

Description: The hitter stands next to the punching bag in his regular stance. The hitter hits the bag powerfully as fast as he can without rest for a determined number of repetitions. This drill can be very demanding, especially if the hitter uses a heavier bat or does a regular rapid-fire drill right after the set with the bag (a rapid-fire drill is when the coach tosses a number of soft tosses or flips in a row without giving the hitter time to rest).

Coaching Point: The hitter can use an old wood bat for this drill.

Drill #28: Hitting a Punching Bag With the Knob of the Bat

Objectives:
- Improves strength
- Teaches hitter to use his hands properly (especially at the beginning of the swing)

Degree of Difficulty: 2B

Equipment Needed:
- A bat
- A punching bag (between 20 and 50 pounds, depending on the hitter's strength)

Description: The hitter sets up in front of the punching bag in his regular stance. The hitter then hits the punching bag with the knob of the bat. To add more difficulty to this drill, the hitter can hold the position for a few seconds. The hitter needs to have a firm grip and strong leg position (back foot on big toe and front leg firm). He should do at least a couple sets of at least 10 repetitions.

Coaching Points:
- The hitter can find punching bags at any sporting goods store or department store.
- The hitter needs to make sure to use his legs and proper mechanics when doing this drill.
- If possible, he should do any of the hitting practices after each set of this drill.

4

Drills That Overload the Hitting Muscles Using Heavier Bats

Drill #29: Swinging a Heavier Bat

Objectives:
- Develops power
- Improves bat speed
- Slows swing down for coaching tips

Degree of Difficulty:
- Dry swings: 1B
- Tee work: 2B
- Soft tosses: 2B
- Flips: 3B
- Batting practice: 3B

Equipment Needed:
- A heavier bat
- A regular bat
- Baseballs
- Batting cage, net, or field

Description: The purpose of this drill is for the hitter to swing a bat heavier than his regular bat. Doing so should make the hitting muscles stronger and quicker. The hitter should use a bat about 6 to 8 ounces heavier than his regular bat to do the overload hitting practice. The hitter can do this drill with the 10-plus-5 approach, swinging 10 times with the heavier bat, and five times with a normal bat.

Coaching Points:
- To develop bat speed, a hitter needs to practice with different weight sizes.
- A heavier bat will make his hitting muscles stronger
- The hitter needs to force himself to swing as fast as he does with his regular bat. This approach is what develops bat speed.
- When picking a heavier bat, the hitter should choose a bat heavy enough to give him a good workout, but not so heavy that he cannot maintain control and do the proper hitting mechanics.
- The hitter should do this drill during the off-season as much as possible.
- The hitter needs to have at least one day in between workouts and should not do this drill as a warm-up before a game, because it will slow him down for the game.

Drill #30: Fast and Slow Swings

Objective: Improves hitting strength

Degree of Difficulty:
- Dry swings: 2B
- With ball involved: 3B

Equipment Needed:
- A heavy bat (or a regular bat with a doughnut or ankle weight)

Description: The hitter uses a heavy bat for this drill (the weight of the bat should be based on the strength of the hitter). The hitter swings fast to his follow-through, pauses, and then rewinds the swing in slow motion back to the starting position. The hitter then repeats until the desired number of reps is done. The hitter can use a ball on a tee also. He swings fast over the ball, trying to knock it down with the wind created by the swing, and then rewinds the swing in slow motion and knocks the ball off the tee. This step will add another dimension to the drill by having the hitter control his body and coordinate his hands.

Coaching Points:
- To maximize intensity, the hitter does this drill doing flips.
- The weight should be at least half a pound all the way to five pounds (ankle weight), depending on the hitter's strength and skill level.

Drill #31: Heavy PVC Swings

Objectives:
- Improves arm strength
- Improves bat speed and power
- Smoothes the swing
- Improves hip flexibility
- Balances out both sides of the body (oblique)

Degree of Difficulty: 2B

Equipment Needed:
- PVC pipe (5 feet long by 1 1/4 inch thick)
- Open space (batting cage, baseball field, open field)

Description: For this drill, the hitter needs a 1 1/4-inch thick by five feet long PVC pipe, which can be bought at any hardware store. Because of the thickness and the length of the pipe, it will feel relatively heavy on the hitter's hands. To do this drill, the hitter stands as he normally does, pointing both feet toward the plate. He then takes a smooth (cutting through the air) swing, trying to keep both feet and the hips pointing to the other side of the plate. The hitter listens to the sound of acceleration of the swing, and only lets the arm extension get the back foot on the big toe (pivot). After 10 swings, the hitter then switches to the other side of the plate (switch-hits). If the hitter is right-handed, he swings left-handed and vice versa. The hitter repeats the drill. When he switch-hits, he will feel how tight his normal front side is because he takes all the swings (rotations) the opposite way. This drill will not only increase the front hip flexibility, but also balance the core area by working the weaker side of his midsection. This drill will also strengthen the hitter's hitting muscles, develop bat speed, and give the hitter feedback of the smoothness and extension of the swing (by the sound). Because of the length and the heaviness of the pipe, the hitter has to finish the swing in order for him not to feel any discomfort during the follow-through.

Variation: Another drill the hitter can do with the PVC pipe is power Vs. For this drill, the hitter grips the pipe as he normally does his regular bat. The hitter then quickly brings the hands down to his belly button and right back up over the front shoulder. The hitter does that 10 times in a row without stopping. After 10 repetitions, the hitter takes a break. After the break, he switches hands (bottom hand goes on top; top hand goes on the bottom) and performs a set that way. A couple of sets would be good to start with. The hitter will feel those forearms burning. Another variation of power Vs is to extend the arms in front of the body, and then mimic a V with the pipe without swinging the arms up and down (hands are kept at the same position for the duration of the drill).

Coaching Points:
- The hitter should listen to the sound of the swing. He needs to hear the acceleration of the swing. It should happen out in front.
- The hitter needs to make sure that he does the other side of the plate (right handed hitter would swing left-handed and vice versa). This is will increase the flexibility of both hips.
- The hitter needs to think fast (swing fast, not hard).

Drill #32: Hitting With a Weighted Doughnut

Objectives:
- Develops power
- Develops bat speed (after the doughnut is taken off the bat)
- Helps coach see hitter's mechanics better because of slower swing

Degree of Difficulty:
- Dry swings: 2B
- Tee work: 2B
- Soft tosses: 3B
- Flips: 3B

Equipment Needed:
- Weighted doughnut
- A bat
- Baseballs
- Batting cage or hitting net
- Optional: Tee

Description: The hitter takes his regular swing with the heavy doughnut on the bat used for warm-up on the on-deck circle. This drill overloads the hitting muscles, making them stronger. The hitter starts by doing dry swings, and then moves on to the next hitting practice (tee, soft tosses, and flips). (Note: This drill should not be performed during batting practice, because of the high risk of the ball ricocheting off the doughnut and injuring the hitter.) To develop bat speed, the hitter then takes a few swings without the doughnut. The hitter should use the 10-plus-5 approach. The hitter takes 10 swings with the doughnut, and five without it. This overload/overspeed program will make the hitter stronger and quicker.

Coaching Points:
- The hitter should take at least a day in between workouts and never do this drill before a game because of the fatigue factor. This drill is great for the off-season.
- To develop bat speed, the hitter needs to give everything he has every time he swings. He should compete against himself to swing faster than the prior swing.

- A doughnut that makes the bat about 25 percent heavier is perfect—somewhere between 6 to 10 ounces, depending on the weight of the bat.
- By not trying to hit the doughnut, the hitter will indirectly use the barrel of the bat better. Making him use the "sweet spot" better.
- The hitter should emphasize intensity instead of contact. The effort is what is important on this drill.
- The hitter should try to find a flat (plastic) doughnut or a small one in a big barrel bat (to leave the sweet spot uncovered). So the ball does not ricochet off of it, and hit the hitter or his partner.
- The hitter needs to take the necessary precautions not to be injured with the heavier weight. He should take hard, but controlled swings.
- Proper rest is as important as the workout itself to prevent fatigue and avoid injury.

Drill #33: Hitting With a Wooden Bat

Objectives:
- Develops power (overload work if the hitter only uses an aluminum bat)
- Teaches the hitter proper hitting mechanics
- Gives the hitter instant feedback of how he has hit the ball
- Develops bat speed (if combined with an aluminum bat)
- Improves bat control (because if he does not hit it correctly, the bat can break)

Degree of Difficulty:
- Dry swing: 1B
- Tee work: 1B
- Soft toss: 1B
- Flips: 2B
- Batting practice: 3B

Equipment Needed:
- A wood bat
- Optional: Aluminum bat
- Baseballs
- Batting cage, hitting net, baseball field, or open space
- A partner
- Optional: Tee

Description: This drill is easy to perform, but difficult to do well. The hitter takes a wood bat and hits with it. This drill is probably the best hitting drill in this manual. A wood bat by itself is probably the best hitting device on the market. It really teaches a hitter how to hit. If the hitter does not follow proper mechanics, he will receive immediate feedback, either by the way it felt in his hands, by the nature of the hit, or by virtue of the fact that the bat broke. If the hitter is dreaming of one day playing professional baseball,

the best advice is for him to start using a wood bat as soon as possible so he gets used to it. If he eventually signs, the transition to wood would be a smooth one.

If the hitter does not hit the ball where he is supposed to hit it (sweet spot), he will know it. On the contrary, using an aluminum bat might give the hitter a wrong idea of what kind of hitter he is. Many hitters do not get drafted because scouts feel that the hitter only has aluminum bat power and that he will not be able to transfer that power to a wood bat. With an aluminum bat, the hitter does not need to hit the ball on the sweet spot to hit the ball pretty hard. Aluminum bats do not break as often, so the hitters are not afraid to get "jammed." The pitchers do not like to throw inside because they are scared the ball will disappear, and because the bat is so much lighter, it helps the hitter produce more bat speed than he typically possesses.

Also, a wood bat makes the hitter stronger. The fact that the balance point is closer to the barrel makes the bat feel heavier than an aluminum bat that is the same weight but that has a balance point closer to the hands. Because of the bat being heavier, the batter's hitting muscles will get stronger over time. When the hitter uses an aluminum bat, he will hit the ball even harder. A wood bat also makes the hitter's hands tougher.

Coaching Points:
- A wood bat could be an expensive investment. If the hitter only uses the wood bat during batting practice and the aluminum during the games, then if/when the wood bat broke, he could nail it back together.
- Taping the barrel where most of the action happens will buy the hitter some time also. It helps protect it from splintering too soon.
- Every time the bat breaks, the hitter can put a few small nails around the break, then tie and nail a strip of rubber from an old bicycle tube. He nails one end above the break, stretches the strip to fasten it as tight as possible, going all the way below the break and nailing that end. Doing so will give the bat even more life.

Drill #34: Wrist Torque

Objectives:
- Improves the way the way the hitter uses his hands on contact (wrist torque)
- Improves bat control and contact
- Improves how the hitter hits through the ball

Degree of Difficulty: 2B

Equipment Needed:
- Bat and baseballs
- Partner and screen

Description: With the ball on the tee, the hitter positions himself with the bat already in the contact position (hands in front of bat, bat head in an angle back to the catcher, eyes on the ball, back knee pointing to the ball, and back foot on big toe). The hitter then creates torque with his hands by pulling the bottom hand back toward the front shoulder and pushing the top hand forward. The hitter tries to isolate the hands, keeping the eyes on the tee (head down). The hitter also tries to finish the swing. This drill is a little frustrating because the ball does not go too far, but besides improving the behavior of the hands on contact, this drill will also strengthen the forearms.

Coaching Point: The regular bat will give the hitter a good workout, but if he needs more resistance, he can use a heavier bat or doughnut on the bat.

Drill #35: Slow-to-Contact, Fast-to-Finish Heavy-Bat Swings

Objectives:
- Improves arm strength and hitting through the ball
- Conditions the hitter

Degree of Difficulty: 2B+ (depending on the weight used)

Equipment Needed:
- Regular bat
- Doughnut, ankle weight, or heavy bat

Description: This drill is another overload drill. The hitter takes the bat from the launching position to the contact position with both arms as slowly as he can. When he reaches the contact position, he explosively takes the bat back to his follow-through. After 10 or so repetitions, the hitter can then do a set of his regular swing with his regular bat.

Coaching Points:
- The weight of the bat will depend on the strength of the hitter.
- The important key of this drill is to control the body-to-arm extension and explode to finish the swing.

Drill #36: Heavy-Bat Drop Ball

Objectives:
- Develops strength
- Develops bat speed
- Improves reaction time
- Improves bat control
- Develops eye-hand coordination

Degree of Difficulty: HR

Equipment Needed:
- A heavy bat (regular bat with doughnut, etc.)
- Baseballs
- Batting cage, hitting net, base field, or open space
- A partner

Description: The hitter stands at home plate as if he has already taken his stride with a bat heavier than what he typically uses. A partner stands at the other side of the plate crossed the hitter. The partner holds a ball about eye level (higher for less experienced hitters). The partner then drops the ball down on a straight line to the plate, without letting the hitter know when he will let go of the ball. The hitter tries to react quickly as soon as he sees the ball, trying to hit it before it hits the ground.

Coaching Points:
- The better the hitter becomes performing this drill, the lower the partner holds the ball before he lets it go.
- The partner needs to stand at a distance so that he will not get hit either by the bat or a hit ball.
- The partner just needs to open his hand up and let go of the ball. He does not need to slam it down to make it go faster. The surprise drop is all the hitter needs to have a good workout.
- The hitter always aims to hit the ball through the middle of the net.
- The hitter needs to be short and quick, but in control, always keeping his eyes at the contact area. He needs to try to see the ball hit the bat.

Drill #37: Heavy-Bat Shapes

Objective: Improves hitting strength by overloading the hitting muscles

Degree of Difficulty: 2B to HR (depending on the weight used)

Equipment Needed:
- Heavy bat or regular bat with doughnut, ankle weight, or weight plate
- Partner with one or two bats
- Open space

Description: Using a heavy bat (doughnut, ankle weight, weight plate, etc.), the hitter does some different motions to strengthen his hands, forearms, and wrists for hitting. This drill can be done with a partner holding one or two bats to show the path the hitter needs to follow, or the hitter can do it by himself by visualizing the path. Each motion should be done in a slow and controlled manner. The hitter needs to reverse the motion and do the opposite arm to maintain symmetry of strength on both arms. Some of the motions the hitter can do include:
- Forced forearm: The hitter uses his bat for this drill (increasing in weight as he gets stronger). The hitter holds his bat with one hand like a hammer. He then sets the bat approximately at a 45-degree angle. The partner in front of the hitter grabs the bat head and tosses it downward (the force depending on the hitter's strength) while the hitter tries to stop the bat head at about waist height. The hitter can also do this drill by himself.

To make it more challenging, the hitter can bring the bat back as quickly as possible to the starting position. The hitter does a set with one arm, and then switches to the other arm.

- Figure eights: The partner stands in front of the hitter with a bat right below the chest and another at about waist height. With his arms extended, the hitter mimics a figure eight only using his hands. The hitter starts with his bat between the partner's two bats, and then goes over the top bat, back to the middle, and below the bottom bat. He then changes directions, following with switching hands.
- Parallel-to-the-ground figure eights: The partner stands in front of the hitter with two bats about shoulder height and width. The hitter starts with the bat in the middle of the two bats and with the arms extended. The hitter then mimics a figure eight only using his hands.

- Pointing-to-the-sky circles: This exercise is done with one arm and a regular bat or two hands and a heavy bat. The hitter extends his arm(s) in front of the body. He then proceeds to do circles just using the wrists. The hitter changes the size of the circles, and all switches the hands to get both arms just as strong.
- Power Vs: The hitter mimics a V.
- Top hand torque: The hitter keeps his hands in front, and then brings the bat head back and forth.
- Triangles: The hitter keeps his hands in front, and then mimics drawing a triangle in the air with the bat.

Coaching Point: The hitter needs to use a weight that is challenging for him to do, but not so heavy that he can only do a couple of reps.

Drill #38: Using a Longer Bat

Objectives:
- Develops power (overloads the hitting muscles because a longer bat is usually heavier)
- Gives a feeling of throwing the hands to the ball and teaches the hitter to use his hands during the swing
- Helps the hitter shorten his swing by forcing him to hit the ball with the barrel of the bat

Degree of Difficulty:
- Dry swings: 2B
- Tee work: 2B
- Soft tosses: 2B
- Flips: 3B
- Batting practice: 3B
- Fungoes: 2B

Equipment Needed:
- Regular bat
- A longer bat
- Baseballs
- Batting cage, hitting net, baseball field, or open space
- Optional: A partner
- Optional: Tee

Description: To perform this drill, the hitter needs to find a bat considerably longer than the one he normally uses. A bat two to five inches longer than his regular bat should be fine, if baseballs are used. For younger hitters, finding a longer bat is easy. For older hitters, it might be a little more difficult because not many hitters use 38- or 40-inch bats anymore. If the

hitter has trouble finding a longer bat, he should consider a stick two to five inches longer than his bat and use tennis balls instead of baseballs.

To do this drill, the hitter takes his normal swing, but makes sure to hit the ball on the sweet spot of the bat (barrel). Because of the length of the bat, this step becomes more difficult to accomplish. To hit the ball on the barrel, the hitter needs to turn the body into the ball while keeping the arms close to the body, and as he makes contact with the ball, the hands go in front of the body to hit through the ball. This action will shorten his swing when he uses his regular bat. Also, a longer bat is usually heavier, so swinging one will make the hitter stronger. This action will transfer to more power.

Coaching Points:
- The trick of doing this drill well is to make a conscious effort to take the barrel right to the ball and hit the ball on the sweet spot of the bat.
- The hitter should swing his regular bat five times after every 10 swings with the longer bat.

Drill #39: Towel Bat

Objectives:
- Teaches hitter the inside-out swing
- Improves wrist action (snap)

Degree of Difficulty: 2B

Equipment Needed:
- A medium-sized towel
- An old wood bat, nails, and a hammer (or an aluminum bat and tape)

Description: First, the hitter puts the towel on the head of the bat according to the type of bat he is using for this drill:
- *Aluminum:* The hitter should tape the towel to the top of the barrel, making sure it is tight enough so that it won't slide off when swinging hard.
- *Old Wood:* The hitter should nail or tape the towel around the top of the barrel, leaving about two thirds of the towel off the bat.

The hitter dry swings as if he has a whip in his hand, trying to get the towel to make a snapping sound (similar to snapping a towel). The louder the sound, the better contact will be. Where the hitter hears the sound is important. The snap should be heard where contact is expected. Right where the hitter needs most of the bat speed.

Coaching Points:
- The hitter needs to use his hands properly for this drill. When a swing is short and quick, he won't hear the towel make as much of a "swish" noise from the beginning of the swing to contact. He just tries to snap it in front of him and follow-through.
- He repeats the swing as many times as possible, trying to snap the towel louder with each subsequent swing. For this muscle-memory drill, repetition is the key.
- The hitter does not use the towel bat as a toy or as a weapon to hit his friends. It could be dangerous to play with it. He needs to make sure nobody is around when he is working with it.

Drill #40: Throwing Bat to the Net

Objectives:
- Improves use of the hands
- Teaches throwing-hands-to-the-ball feeling

Degree of Difficulty: 2B

Equipment Needed:
- A bat (preferably wood)
- A batting cage

Description: The hitter gets three to five feet in front of the net, although some hitters like to do it on an open field just to challenge themselves with throwing the bat farther than the prior throw. The hitter takes his normal swing, but instead of finishing it with a follow-through, he lets go of the bat right before he is about to roll his wrists over. The hitter should work on doing this drill with inside, outside, high, and low pitches. He should do 10 or more throws, then take some soft tosses or any kind of hitting practice and feel his hands just go to the ball.

Coaching Points:
- Some coaches teach their hitters how to finish their swings by letting go of the bat after the follow-through. If your hitters have that problem, try this approach; it might help.
- The hitter should make sure that the net is not too tight where it could bounce back and hit him.
- The hitter needs to make sure to check if any people are around while he is doing the drill.
- Drill can be used as a warm-up.

Drill #41: Cut the Tree

Objectives:
- Improves arm extension on contact
- Teaches the arms how to work during the swing
- Strengthens the arms and shoulders for hitting
- Improves bat speed and contact

Degree of Difficulty:
- With regular bat: 1B
- With heavy bat: 2B

Equipment Needed:
- Baseballs
- A bat
- Batting cage or baseball field
- Optional: Tee, partner, heavy bat, doughnut

Description: To make this drill more realistic, the hitter can put a towel or a similar object between his back shoulder and his shirt to rise up his starting point. This drill can be done three ways:
- The hitter stands with his bat over his head with the elbows flexed. The hitter then brings the bat forcefully forward over the head, by straightening the elbows out and stopping the bat at chest level. The hitter does not use his shoulder, but relies only on extending the elbows, just as he would do on contact.
- The hitter stands with his bat on his back shoulder with his elbows flexed. The hitter then brings his bat forcefully in front of him, by extending his arms at the elbows, stopping at chest high.
- The hitter rolls each one of the towels inside his shirt on his shoulders. The hitter stands with his bat on his back shoulder with his elbows flexed. The hitter then brings his bat forcefully in front of him by extending his arms at the elbows, stopping at chest height, but instead of stopping his bat at that position, he explosively brings the bat up to the other shoulder. He will be forming a "V." He needs to make sure that he only uses his arms during this drill, and only extends the elbows.

Coaching Points:
- The hitter should do five regular swings after every set of 10 ax swings that he performs.
- The hitter can make this drill even tougher by adding a heavy doughnut to the bat or using a heavier bat.
- The hitter should stretch his arms and shoulders properly before engaging in this drill.

Drill #42: Hitting Fungoes With a Heavy Bat

Objectives:
- Improves hitting mechanics
- Strengthens the hitter
- Improves bat control

Degree of Difficulty: 3B

Equipment Needed:
- A heavier-than-normal bat
- Baseballs
- Batting cage, field, or net
- Optional: Fielder

Description: The idea of this drill is to have the hitter practice his swing as if he were hitting grounders to an infielder but using a heavier bat instead of a fungo. The hitter tosses the ball to himself with either arm, but makes sure that he keeps as close to proper mechanics as possible without losing his balance during the sequence of the swing. He can do this drill in front of a net if he is by himself or when his team is taking batting practice.

Coaching Points:
- This drill is great for improving his mechanics. It is like an action tee. He has to see the ball all the way, keep the head down, swing down (short and quick), swing through the ball, and he can't overswing if he wants to hit grounders.
- The hitter should use his bottom hand to toss the ball to himself.
- The hitter needs to try to mimic a good swing every time.
- If the hitter does this drill during batting practice, he needs to make sure he hits the grounder right after the player at the plate hits the ball and not at the same time. This technique will protect the fielder from getting hit by either ball.

Drill #43: Self-Toss One-Arm Swings

Objective: Improves the way the hitter uses each arm hands during the swing

Degree of Difficulty: 2B

Equipment Needed:
- Small bat and baseballs
- Batting cage or hitting net

Description: The hitter stands as he normally would at his stance with a ball in his bottom hand and the little or choked-up bat on the top hand. The hitter then tosses the ball to himself (around the hitting zone) and as the ball is coming down, he turns his back side—pivoting the back foot and the back shoulder, keeping his eyes on the ball—and hits it right back to the net. After a few swings, he switches hands. To make this drill more challenging, he can close one of his eyes or he can wear a wrist weight.

Coaching Point: This drill will also help the hitter track the ball, keep his head down, and strengthen each arm.

Drill #44: Slow-Motion Hitting Position on Contact

Objective: Improves hitting position on contact

Degree of Difficulty: 2B

Equipment Needed:
- Baseballs and heavy or regular bat
- Tee
- Partner

Description: The coach places a ball on a tee in different contact locations. The hitter then goes through his swing in slow motion, trying to take the bat head to the ball. The hitter stops before he hits the ball and freezes. The coach then checks the position of the hitter on contact and tells him if he is in a good position or needs to make an adjustment. The different locations are high, low, middle, in, and out (and a combination of these). If the hitter is in a strong contact position, the hitter then explosively swings the bat hitting the ball to a net. The hitter should master this drill with his regular bat before adding weight to the bat. A heavier bat or doughnut will challenge the hitter to get stronger. Another way to increase the level of difficulty is by holding on the contact position for a count of five, and then hit the ball.

Coaching Points:
- The contact position should look something like this:
- The front leg is firm.
- The back leg looks like a backward "L."
- The eyes are looking at the ball.
- The back arm is flexed with the fingers pointing up.
- The front arm is straight (or almost straight) with the fingers pointing down.
- The navel is pointing to the ball.
- After a set of this drill, the hitter can do his regular swing, trying to get to that proper contact position but making sure he finishes his swing properly.

Drill #45: Heavy-Bat Self-Serve

Objectives:
- Develops power
- Strengthens the hitter

Degree of Difficulty: 3B or HR (depending on the weight of the bat)

Equipment Needed:
- A heavier-than-normal bat
- Baseballs
- Baseball field or open space

Description: The hitter stands at home plate of a baseball field with a bat that is heavier than his regular bat. The hitter holds a ball with his top hand and the bat with his bottom hand. The hitter then tosses the ball to himself and tries to hit the ball out of the park on a line drive. The hitter provides all the power, so by putting everything into the swing and using a heavier bat, he will be able to get stronger, thus helping him to hit the ball harder. This drill will give the hitter tremendous extension, plus get his hitting muscles stronger.

Coaching Points:
- The hitter needs to use all parts of the field to challenge himself and not groove his swing to one location.
- The hitter needs to try to better himself each time. He has to compete against himself or a friend to make it more fun. Hard work is the key.
- If players are on the field, the hitter needs to let them know what he is doing so they pay attention and do not get hit by the ball.

Drill #46: Metal Pipe Contact

Objectives:
- Improves strength
- Improves contact and eye-hand coordination

Degree of Difficulty:
- Flips: 2B
- Batting practice: 3B

Equipment Needed:
- 1/4-inch metal pipe (length = bat size)
- Tape
- Baseball
- Batting cage

Description: The hitter prepares the pipe with a handle and a knob so the pipe does not slip. The partner then tosses balls to the hitter, and the hitter tries to make contact with an object that has a significantly smaller diameter than his regular bat. The weight of the metal bat will more than likely be heavier than the hitter's regular bat. This aspect makes this drill not only an eye-hand coordination drill, but also an overloading drill. This smaller diameter will make contact more challenging and will force the hitter to concentrate on following the ball all the way to the contact area.

Coaching Points:
- The hitter can use pipes of varying diameters.
- The metal pipes can be bought at any hardware store.

Drill #47: Heavy-Bat Slow-Motion Swing Progression

Objectives:
- Improves arm and hitting strength
- Conditions the hitter

Degree of Difficulty: 2B+ (depending on the weight used)

Equipment Needed:
- Regular bat
- Doughnut, ankle weight, or heavy bat

Description: This overload drill can significantly strengthen the hitter and can be done at home, especially during the off-season. The different ways this drill can be done are as follows:
- The hitter goes in slow motion from beginning to end, bringing the bat back with normal speed, in slow motion, and as fast as he can.
- The hitter can also bring the bat back in slow motion, but this time he swings his regular bat without the weight as fast as he can. One heavy and one regular swing combination is one repetition.
- The hitter goes in slow motion from beginning to end, bringing the bat back, does five wrist torques, and then brings the bat back in slow motion.

After 10 or so repetitions, the hitter can then do a set of his regular swings with his regular bat.

Coaching Points:
- The weight of the bat will depend on the strength of the hitter.
- The important key of this drill is to control the body.

Drill #48: Slow One-Handed Swings

Objectives:
- Improves arm strength
- Improves swing path
- Shortens the swing by making the hitter aware of what he is doing
- Improves balance

Degree of Difficulty: 2B+ (depending on the weight used)

Equipment Needed:
- Small or regular bat
- Doughnut, ankle weight, or heavy bat

Description: This overload drill also isolates each arm. The hitter does a slow-motion swing with a weighted bat (weight on bat head). The hitter needs to go from beginning to end as slow as he can, using his front arm first and then his back arm. After each set, the hitter can do a slow-motion swing with both hands, and then a set of his regular swing with his regular bat.

Coaching Points:
- The weight of the bat will depend on the strength of the hitter. This drill requires body control, so it is preferable for the hitter to use a lighter weight and do the drill correctly rather than using a heavier weight and not having any balance.
- This drill will not only work on arm strength, but also on balance and body coordination.

Drill #49: Double Weight on the Bat

Objectives:
- Develops power
- Improves bat speed
- Shows hitter how to use his hands during the swing

Degree of Difficulty:
- Dry swings: 2B
- Tee work: 2B
- Soft tosses: 2B
- Flips: 3B

Equipment Needed:
- Smaller ankle weight (1 pound or less)
- Heavier ankle weight (3 pounds or less)
- Bat
- Tape
- Baseballs
- Batting cage, net, or field

Description: The hitter tapes the smaller ankle weight around the knob of the bat and the heavier weight on the handle. The double weight bat will show the hitter how to use his hands properly while at the same time making him stronger. This drill helps to make the hitting muscles stronger and quicker. The hitter can do this drill with the 10-plus-5 approach, swinging 10 times with the heavier bat and five times with his normal bat.

Coaching Points:
- The hitter needs to force himself to swing as fast as he does with his regular bat. This action is what develops bat speed.
- The hitter should do this drill during the off-season as much as possible.
- The hitter needs to have at least one day in between workouts and should not do this drill before a game, because it will slow him down for the game.
- This bat can be used in the on-deck circle as a warm-up before at-bats.

5

Drills That Overload the Hitting Muscles Using Heavier Balls

Drill #50: Hitting a Basketball off the Tee

Objectives:
- Teaches hitter how to drive the ball
- Improves power and hitting strength

Degree of Difficulty: 3B

Equipment Needed:
- Tee
- Bat and basketball
- Backstop or open field

Description: For this drill, the hitter needs a basketball and a tee. The hitter sets up the tee in front of the backstop if he is working by himself or facing an open space if he has somebody retrieving the balls. The hitter places the ball on the tee. The hitter then hits the ball, giving it backspin (to drive the ball). The lines of the basketball show the hitter which rotation the ball has.

Coaching Point: To hit the ball with backspin, the hitter needs to make contact with the bat at an angle back and hit through the bottom of the ball.

Drill #51: Hitting a Deflated Basketball

Objectives:
- Develops power (overload)
- Develops bat speed (overspeed)
- Develops explosiveness and stronger contact

Degree of Difficulty: 3B

Equipment Needed:
- A bat
- A deflated basketball (or soccer ball, or volleyball)
- Open space
- Optional: Baseballs

Description: The hitter lets about half of the air out of an old basketball or any similar size ball. He needs to make sure that no bounce is left in the ball. He can test it by trying to bounce it off the floor. A partner tosses it to the hitter as an underhand flip from about 15 feet away. The hitter takes his normal swing, putting total effort on every one of them.

This drill is another overload drill. It helps the hitter become stronger by hitting an object that is significantly heavier than a regular baseball. This drill also becomes a bat-speed drill when the hitter hits a regular baseball after hitting the basketball. The difference in size gives the hitter a surprising extra power he does not realize he possesses.

Coaching Points:
- The most important thing about this drill is that the basketball needs to have no bounce at all. If the ball still has any bounce, when the hitter hits the ball, the bat can come back and hit the player in the face.
- The hitter should try to follow the 10-plus-5 routine. After every 10 swings with the basketball, the hitter should take five swings with some regular baseballs.

Drill #52: Hitting Old Balls Overload

Objectives:
- Strengthens the hitting muscles
- Teaches the hitter to put maximum effort on every swing because the balls do not go anywhere
- Develops bat speed

Degree of Difficulty:
- Long flips: 2B
- Batting practice: 2B

Equipment Needed:
- Old balls
- A bat
- A feeder
- A screen
- Batting cage or baseball field
- Optional: Newer balls

Description: Old, raggedy balls should not be thrown away, but instead should be used for a drill. Understandably, old balls do not go as far as newer balls, but that is the idea. This drill is another overload drill, which makes the hitter stronger, because the balls are heavier than the regular balls.

The hitter takes his normal swing, hitting the old balls (the worse their condition, the better) as hard or far as he can. The balls will not go as far, so the hitter needs to put everything he has on every swing. This drill is only done with flips, soft tosses, or batting practice pitches and preferably on an open field.

Coaching Points:
- With this drill, the hitter can see the difference right away of the 10-plus-5 routine. He should hit 10 old balls as hard and far as he can, then hit five newer balls. The hitter will see how the ball just jumps of his bat.
- The hitter needs to remember to recycle his baseballs. The worse the condition of the ball, the better they are for this drill.
- Competing with a friend will make this drill more fun.

Drill #53: Hitting Softballs Overload

Objectives:
- Strengthens the hitting muscles
- Improves contact and bat speed
- Improves bat speed if this drill is combined with regular baseballs

Degree of Difficulty:
- Long, soft tosses: 2B
- Flips: 3B
- Batting practice: 3B

Equipment Needed:
- As many softballs as possible
- Baseballs
- A bat
- A feeder
- A screen
- Batting cage or baseball field

Description: The concept on overloading is very simple: to get the muscles bigger and stronger, a person needs to increase the load with which those muscles work. If the weight is kept the same, the muscles will get used to it, and they will not get stronger. In other words, if the hitter practices hitting something heavier than a baseball, his hitting muscles will get stronger and he will hit the ball harder. One way to overload the hitting muscles is by hitting softballs. Softballs are heavier than baseballs, and they do not go as far. Hitting softballs during batting practice, flips, or long soft tosses will help the hitter get stronger. The hitter will see a real difference if he hits a few baseballs after a set of hitting softballs. The baseball will seem to jump off the bat.

Coaching Points:
- Softballs are indeed heavier than baseballs and do not go as far, but the hitter should not get discouraged. He has to remember that the baseball will be lighter and will therefore travel farther.
- The heavier and softer the softballs are, the better they are for this drill.

Drill #54: Hitting Heavy Balls Overload

Objectives:
- Strengthens the hitting muscles
- Helps the hitter to hit the ball harder
- Improves power and bat speed

Degree of Difficulty:
- Soft tosses: 2B
- Flips: 3B

Equipment Needed:
- Heavy baseballs
- Regular baseballs
- A bat
- A feeder
- Batting cage or baseball field
- A screen

Description: The concept on overloading is very simple: to get the muscles bigger and stronger, a person needs to increase the load with which those muscles work. If the weight is kept the same, the muscles will get used to it. They will not get stronger. In other words, if the hitter practices hitting something heavier than a baseball, his hitting muscles will get stronger, and he will hit the ball harder. Hitting heavy balls should only be done with flips and soft tosses practice.

Coaching Points:
- Heavy balls do not go as far as baseballs, but the hitter will notice how the baseball starts going farther the more he practices with these heavy balls.
- The hitter needs to hold the bat a little tighter than when he is hitting regular balls because the heavy balls are tougher on the hands.
- Encourage your players to do the following program:
  ✓ 10 swings with heavy balls and regular bat
  ✓ 10 swings with regular balls and regular bat
- The best heavy balls to hit are PWR Baseballs (www.pwrbaseball.com).

Drill #55: Hitting Wet Balls

Objective: Improves hitting strength by overloading hitting muscles

Degree of Difficulty:
- Flips: 2B
- Batting practice: 2B

Equipment Needed:
- Bucket and water
- Old balls
- Old wood or metal bat

Description: The hitter sets a few old balls in a bucket of water for a while (depending on how heavy he wants the ball to get). He then takes them out and lets them dry. The hitter then hits those balls using either soft tosses or flips. The added weight will overload the hitting muscles and help the hitter get stronger in a systematic approach to hitting. After a few repetitions, the hitter can hit some regular balls to add the extra power to his swing.

Coaching Points:
- Heavy balls can be bought from online retailers.
- The hitter needs to make sure to use an old wood or metal bat for this drill.

6

Drills That Overload the Hitting Muscles Using Different Resistances

Drill #56: Swinging Inside the Pool

Objectives:
- Develops power (overload)
- Develops bat speed (overspeed)
- Functions as a therapeutic hitting program
- Develops hip flexibility
- Cleans the swing of extra movement (makes the swing more efficient)

Degree of Difficulty: 2B

Equipment Needed:
- A bat (preferably an old wood one)
- A swimming pool (shallow end)

Description: If the hitter has access to a swimming pool, he needs to take advantage of it. To do this drill, he gets inside the pool, where the water is about shoulder high (shallow end). Depending on how much resistance he wants, he starts his hands:
- Outside the water for more
- Inside the water for less

He should experiment to see which works better for him. Then, he takes his normal swing, making an effort to finish the swing (follow through). The faster the swing, and the lighter the bat, the more resistance the water will apply to his swing. This drill will

strengthen his hitting muscles, without making him feel too fatigued at the end of the workout.

Variations:
- He can also swing with one arm at a time.
- With the bat inside the water about waist or chest high (experiment), the hitter can swing the bat back and forth as if performing half circles in front of himself. He should use his arms, keeping the feet planted on the floor of the pool. He should swing as hard backward as he would forward (like rewinding his swing).
- The hitter should touch the floor of the pool with the end of the bat, and then bring the bat out of the water in a vertical line as fast as he can. He should do this move a few times, and then switch hands (top to bottom and bottom to top) to even out the work.

Coaching Points:
- If the hitter has enough room, he should swing the bat in the water 10 to 15 times, then get out of the pool and swing five times as fast as he can to increase his bat speed.
- The hitter should take at least one day in between workouts.
- If the hitter is injured, this drill could complement a rehab program (but consult with a trainer first).
- The hitter should keep in mind that he is in the water. He should take the necessary precautions, including checking if a lifeguard is on duty or bringing a friend.
- Other people might be swimming around the hitter, so he should make sure he has a lot of open space to swing the bat without jeopardizing others.

Drill #57: Resist-a-Bat

Objectives:
- Develops power (overload)
- Develops bat speed (overspeed)

Degree of Difficulty: 2B (depending on the resistance)

Equipment Needed:
- A bat
- A partner

Description: This drill makes the hitter stronger by providing resistance in different locations of the swing path, providing isometric resistance to the swing. It can be done two ways:
- A partner holds the barrel of the bat as the hitter is performing a slow-motion swing. The partner gives the hitter resistance at different stages of the swing, holding the bat for a count or providing continuous resistance as the hitter goes through the swing. The hitter just tries to overcome the resistance of the partner. The resistance should not be either too hard or too soft (experiment). Greater emphasize should be devoted to the area right before contact.

- If the hitter is by himself, he can utilize a sturdy, immovable object such as a column or a tree for the purpose of this drill. He lets that object provide the resistance, while he moves himself around so he can work on different parts of his swing. The hitter will not be able to have continuous resistance throughout the swing, but he will be able to pick a spot on his swing and hold for 5 to 10 seconds, and then move to another location.

Coaching Points:
- The hitter needs to remember that this drill is not a swing.
- If necessary, the partner can use both of his hands in front of his chest to resist stronger hitters.
- This exercise is a drill, not a game. The hitter cannot do anything foolish which could jeopardize the partner's health.
- After every session, the hitter should take a couple swings for bat speed and swing feel.
- The hitter should do this drill will at least one day of rest in between, and never right before a game.
- This drill is great for younger hitters.

Drill #58: Partner Resistance Competition

Objectives:
- Improves arm strength
- Improves hitting through the ball
- Improves arm extension

Degree of Difficulty:
- Regular (wood) bat: 2B
- Heavy bat: 2B (depends on weight)

Equipment Needed:
- Regular bat or heavy bat
- Partner

Description: The hitter starts this drill with his regular, bat but the goal is for him to use a heavier bat (and the bat used should be increasingly heavier). A teammate or partner stands at the other side of home plate with a bat. Both hitters put the bats in the contact area as if they were touching to swords. They then resist each other, trying to push the other bat back. Each set should last at least 10 seconds.

Coaching Point: The heavier the bat, the better, but the key should be control.

Drill #59: Heavy Bat Plus Resistance

Objectives:
- Improves arm strength
- Improves hitting through the ball
- Improves arm extension

Degree of Difficulty: 2B

Equipment Needed:
- Regular bat
- Heavy bat or bat with doughnut or ankle weight
- Partner with bat or pipe

Description: The hitter starts this drill with his regular bat, but the goal is for him to use a heavier bat (as he gets stronger, the bat used should be increasingly heavier). An adult partner stands at the other side of home plate with a bat or long PVC pipe in one or both hands, depending on the strength of the hitter. The hitter puts the bat head on the contact area, and the partner holds his bat out as if it is a ball. The partner then resists the hitter, while the hitter pushes through the resistance. When the hitter gets to the power V position (arm extension), he has two choices: either stop at that point, go back, and do another repetition, or react quickly by taking the bat to his finish position as soon as the partner takes his bat off the hitter's bat.

Coaching Points:
- The heavier the bat, the better, but the key should be control.
- The hitter can use a heavier bat, use a doughnut on the bat, use a heavy metal pipe, tape pennies on the bat head, use an ankle weight on the bat head, and so forth.

Drill #60: Isometric Power

Objectives:
- Strengthens the hitter
- Improves power
- Improves contact and hand strength

Degree of Difficulty: 2B

Equipment Needed:
- A pole or immobile object
- A bat
- Open space or baseball field
- Optional: Baseballs, feeder, screen, tee

Description: The hitter uses a strong, sturdy pole or other immobile object for this drill. This drill should be for older hitters. The hitter gets in front of the object with his bat in his hands. The hitter then goes to different parts of the swing, pushing the object with the bat. He holds the position, starting with 15 seconds and going all the way to 60 seconds. After he has done one location (for example the contact area) for a period of time, he rests and repeats or changes locations.

Coaching Points:
- The hitter should emphasize the contact area, especially at different pitch locations (in, out, up, down, etc.). Other areas of push and hold can be the start of the swing, using the knob to push down to the front foot, as well as during the path of the swing, and after contact so the hitter is strong through the ball.
- The hitter needs to push away hard in the contact area to mimic hitting through the ball.
- At the contact area, the hitter needs to have his "palm up, palm down" position and push hard away, feeling the resistance in the hands and forearms. Also, the front arm needs to be extended with the back arm in an "L" shape.

Drill #61: Isometric Push Back

Objectives:
- Improves arm strength for hitting
- Improves core area strength

Degree of Difficulty: 2B

Equipment Needed:
- Bat
- Pole, tree, or concrete corner

Description: The hitter stands in front of a strong pole, tree, or concrete corner. He then proceeds (using an old wood bat, if possible) to set up the bat on the object as if he is making contact with a ball. He then pushes himself back while having the back foot slightly off the ground. The front leg is the anchor, and the back foot just goes back for a ride.

Coaching Points:
- The hitter needs to make sure that he is pushing all the way to forming a V with his arms.
- The hitter also needs to make sure that he is not pushing himself back (by adding momentum) but allowing the arms to do all the work.
- This drill will also stabilize the core area. A variation of the drill is to do it on a wheeled office chair.

Drill #62: Holding Position to Improve Front-Hip Flexibility

Objectives:
- Improves front hip flexibility
- Improves balance

Degree of Difficulty: 2B

Equipment Needed:
- A clock
- A bat
- An open space

Description: The hitter does a couple of sets of the following stances to improve front hip coordination:
- With the bat in his stance position
- With the bat in his launching position after taking his stride
- With the bat in the contact position with his front foot closed and pointing to the plate, and the back foot shoelaces pointing to the pitcher

- With the bat in the follow-through position with his front foot closed and pointing to the plate, and the back foot shoelaces pointing to the pitcher

The hitter tries to hold each position for at least 30 seconds. As he gets better, the hitter keeps turning the front foot inwardly until the front toes are almost pointing to the back foot. As the front hip gets more flexible, the hitter will see how he can swing with more power.

Coaching Points:
- The hitter needs to try to keep from shaking.
- To help himself, the hitter can use a heavy obstacle to keep the front foot closed.
- A heavier bat can be used, and the hitter can increase the time that he holds the position to improve muscle memory and balance.

Drill #63: Walking Partner Resistance Swing

Objective: Improves hitting strength by overloading the hitting muscles

Degree of Difficulty: 2B

Equipment Needed:
- Bat
- Partner
- Open space

Description: The partner stands next to the hitter with one hand on the bat head and the other hand on the handle. The hitter starts pulling the bat while the partner resists him with the top hand. As the hitter is completing the swing, the resistance goes from the top hand to the hand on the handle. The partner walks around the hitter as the hitter is finishing the swing, giving enough resistance to force the hitter to work hard and get stronger.

Coaching Point: The partner should offer enough resistance, making sure that the hitter can do his swing properly with no mechanical break down.

Drill #64: Starting the Swing

Objectives:
- Teaches the hitter to properly start his swing
- Teaches the hitter to keep the head stable during the start of the swing
- Shows the coach how the hitter is starting his swing (arms or shoulders), then allows him to make the necessary adjustment

Degree of Difficulty: 1B

Equipment Needed:
- A bat
- A coach or adult
- An open field

Description: This drill is used for younger hitters to teach them how to properly start the swing. The coach has the important role in this drill. If the hitter is right-handed, the coach uses his right hand to hold the bat, and if he is left-handed, the coach uses his left hand to hold the bat.

The hitter (right-handed for the explanation of the drill) takes his stance, and the coach holds the bat with his right hand and the hitter's head with his left hand. The coach holds the bat firmly so the bat does not slip from his hand. The coach then tells the hitter to start his swing. The coach holds the head still and the bat back. The coach then sees how the hitter is pulling the bat forward (arms or shoulders) and to where he is pulling (down to the ground or away from him). The coach makes him do this drill until he feels that the hitter is pulling the bat correctly. After he is doing it correctly, the hitter takes a few swings with soft tosses or flips. The coach repeats the drill when he sees the hitter not pulling the bat properly.

Coaching Points:
- The coach needs to make sure to hold the bat firmly so the hitter does not let go and hit him.
- The coach needs to remind the hitter that he is not swinging but just working on the start of the swing, so he does not hit the coach on the follow-through.
- The hitter needs to do some live swings to transfer the feeling of the drill to his swing.

Drill #65: Exercise Ball Between Legs

Objectives:
- Improves power by teaching hitter to use legs properly
- Improves leg strength

Degree of Difficulty:
- Dry swings: 1B
- Tee work: 1B
- Soft tosses: 2B
- Flips: 2B

Equipment Needed:
- A deflated exercise ball (Swiss ball)
- A bat

Description: The hitter sets the ball between his legs (thighs). The hitter goes through his swing by pinching the back knee toward the other leg and squeezing the ball powerfully. If the legs are not squeezed, then the ball will drop. The hitter needs to make sure to get the front leg firm (avoiding lunging, with the front knee bending forward toward the pitcher).

Coaching Points:
- This drill is great for teaching the hitter how to use the legs properly.
- The size of the ball should depend on the size of the hitter.
- These balls can be bought from many sporting goods stores, department stores, and online retailers.

Drills That Overload the Hitting Muscles Using Exercise or Surgical Tubing

Drill #66: Tubing Swing

Objective: Strengthens the midsection for rotational power

Degree of Difficulty: 2B

Equipment Needed:
- Rubber tubing
- A steady place to fasten the tubing (like a pole or a door)

Description: The hitter fastens one end of the tubing around a pole or something similar up over his head and then holds the other end of the tubing with his other hand. Or, to make the drill more hitting-specific, the hitter can attach the other end of the tubing through a hole in a PVC pipe, dowel, or wood bat handle to feel the grip of the bat during the drill. The hitter then mimics his swing down. For more resistance, the hitter goes away from the object and for less he goes closer to it. The hitter can also do the same basic form, but he puts the tubing around something down on the ground, and swings up to strengthen other muscles of the midsection and obliques.

Coaching Points:
- The hitter needs to make sure to check the tubing for cracks and scrapes so the tubing does not break during use. Tubing is more flexible than cable swing.
- The tubing can be bought at any sporting goods or department store. They are available in different levels of resistance and can be used for working out and for rehab.
- The drill can be used by younger hitters.

Drill #67: Tubing-Around-the-Back Extension

Objectives:
- Improves arm extension
- Strengthens the arms for hitting

Degree of Difficulty: 2B

Equipment Needed:
- Tubing
- Optional: A bat

Description: The hitter uses exercise tubing to improve arm extension and to strengthen the arms for the swing. The hitter wraps each end of the tubing on each hand and sets the loop (the rest of the tubing) behind his back, making sure that it is tight enough to give him good resistance. The hitter then extends his arm as if he is swinging. He can either do a set of slow reps, or like his regular swing, or 10 swings as fast as he can. The hitter can either stop at extension or finish his swing and complete his follow-through.

Coaching Points:
- After each set, the hitter can take five regular swings.
- The hitter needs to make sure that the tubing has no cracks or breaks so he does not hurt himself.
- The hitter should also use tubing of different levels of resistance.

Drill #68: Tubing Around the Back Shoulder, Front-Arm Extension

Objectives:
- Improves use of front arm (beginning of swing)
- Strengthens front arm

Degree of Difficulty: 2B

Equipment Needed:
- Tubing
- Optional: A bat

Description: This drill is done to improve the use and strength of the front arm. It also helps correct casting of the front arm (front arm extends prematurely). The hitter uses exercise tubing, holding the two ends with his front hand, and putting the loop around his back shoulder (the tubing should not be hanging). The hitter then extends the arm as if he was swinging. He can do slow repetitions, or fast ones. The hitter stops at extension if he is doing dry swings, or he can do swing bunts (i.e., he just taps the ball and stops at the contact location).

Coaching Points:
- After each set, the hitter can take five regular swings.
- The hitter needs to make sure that the tubing has no cracks or breaks so he does not hurt himself.
- The hitter should also use tubing of different levels of resistance.

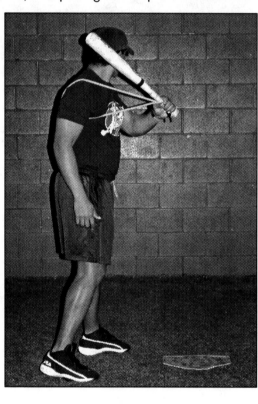 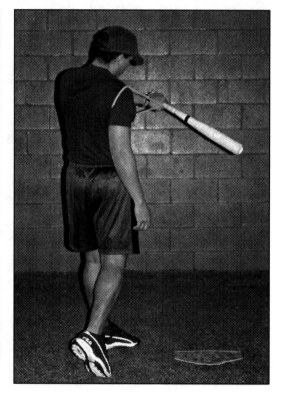

Drill #69: Tubing Around the Front Shoulder

Objectives:
- Improves loading (taking the hands back)
- Strengthens arms for hitting

Degree of Difficulty: 2B

Equipment Needed:
- Tubing
- Optional: A bat

Description: This drill is done to improve the way the hitter loads up (takes the hands back). It also strengthens the arms to hit the ball harder. The hitter uses exercise tubing by looping it around his front shoulder and holding it in one of the following ways:

- The two ends with his top hand
- Each end with each hand
- The tubing between the bat handle and the hands

The hitter then extends the tubing as if it was a slingshot. He can then do slow repetitions and go through his swing, or he can just hold at launching position for as long as he can.

Coaching Points:
- After each set, the hitter can take five regular swings.
- The hitter needs to make sure that the tubing has no cracks or breaks so he does not hurt himself.
- The hitter should also use tubing of different levels of resistance.

Drill #70: Belt and Tubing Drifting and Rotation

Objectives:
- Helps get rid of drifting
- Teaches proper balance after stride
- Strengthens rotation

Degree of Difficulty:
- Dry swings 1B
- Tee work: 1B
- Soft tosses: 2B
- Flips: 2B

Equipment Needed:
- A belt
- A piece of surgical or exercise tubing
- Bat and baseballs
- Batting cage
- Pole to tie tubing

Description: For this drill, the hitter ties the tubing around the belt. He ties the belt around his waist with one end of the rope on the back hip, and the other end of the tubing tied to a strong pole or something that would not give. The hitter moves forward until the tubing is fully or almost fully stretched, depending on whether or not he strides up and down or steps forward.

The idea is for the hitter to take his swing without stretching the tubing too much at the beginning of the swing, but feeling the turning of the body during the rotation. In other words, he should not feel the tubing pulling him back horizontally but he feeling the resistance as he is turning his backside to the ball.

Coaching Points:
- The hitter needs to do this drill often to give his body the muscle memory to get rid of drifting (the sliding of the hips during the swing).
- The hitter needs to make sure that the tubing is safe to use (no cuts or scrapes).

Drill #71: Belt and Tubing Rotation

Objectives:
- Improves power by improving rotation
- Teaches proper balance after stride
- Strengthens rotation

Degree of Difficulty:
- Hitting punching bag: 2B
- High pitches: 2B

Equipment Needed:
- A belt
- A piece of surgical or exercise tubing
- A bat
- Punching bag

Description: For this drill, the hitter ties the belt around his waist with one end of the rope on the back hip, and the other end of the tubing tied to the bottom of a strong pole or something similar. Then, the hitter moves away from where the tubing is tied up until the tubing is fully or almost fully stretched. Hitting a tire or a punching bag is recommended, but this drill can be done with high flips or soft tosses (so the hitter does not hit the tubing during the swing).

The hitter then takes his swing. The tubing will pull him to the punching bag, which will force him to swing faster. Trying to hold his balance will allow the hitter to strengthen his core area and improve his balance.

Coaching Points:
- The hitter can do this drill often to give his body the muscle memory to swing faster.
- The hitter needs to make sure that the tubing is safe to use (no cuts or scrapes).

Drill #72: Tubing on Bat Barrel

Objectives:
- Improves arm strength
- Improves wrist torque

Degree of Difficulty: 2B

Equipment Needed:
- A bat
- Tubing
- Partner

Description: The hitter can use an old bat and tape the end of a strip of elastic tubing to the barrel. The other end of the tubing is either secured to a door or something similar, or by an adult who stands away from the hitter, giving him enough resistance to give the hitter a good hand-forearm workout. The hitter can do this drill either by using or not using his feet. When not using the feet, the arms will work harder.

Following are a couple variations:
- The hitter starts with his arms extended in the power V position, then takes the top hand forward and backward in slow motion (keeping the arms extended and the cord stretched).
- The hitter can do an explosive movement forward, and then bring the bat head back in slow motion for double work.
- The hitter can do 10 repetitions as fast as he can.

Coaching Points:
- The hitter does not roll his wrists, but just works on stretching the cord only using his hands.
- The hitter needs to check the tubing for cuts and scrapes so the tubing does not snap.
- The partner stands at different positions so the hitter can mimic swinging at pitches at different locations.

Drill #73: Tubing on Knob and Handle

Objective: Improves hitting strength by overloading the hitting muscles

Degree of Difficulty: 2B

Equipment Needed:
- A bat
- Exercise or surgical tubing

Description: The hitter needs exercise or surgical tubing for this drill. The hitter secures one end of the tubing to something low (chain-link fence, bottom of the door, etc.). He then takes one of the tubing's other handles and tapes it around the bat head, and he either holds the other handle with the bottom hand or tapes it around the knob. He first pulls the tubing around the handle in a slow and controlled manner, keeping the bat head back. After the bottom hand cannot go any longer, he starts extending the tubing on the bat head, holding in his power V position (arm extended, front leg firm, and back foot on the big toe with shoelaces pointing to the pitcher) or keeps going until he is pointing the end of the bat over the center fielder's head. At this position, he holds for five seconds then goes back to the starting position and repeats for five repetitions.

Coaching Points:
- The hitter needs to make sure that the tubing does not have cuts or scratches.
- The best way to do this drill is by having one of those handles that wrap around instead of the hard handle, but the hard handle can work if the hitter holds the handle with his thumb during the handle sets and is careful with the other sets by doing the set very slowly so the handle does not slide down (a big head bat usually works well). For the bat head drill, the hitter can tape the handle if he has an old bat that he is not using much.

Drill #74: Tubing Around the Back Knee, Back-Leg Pivot

Objectives:
- Teaches the hitter how to pivot the back leg properly
- Improves power by strengthening the back leg pivot

Degree of Difficulty:
- Dry swings: 2B
- Tee work: 2B
- Soft tosses: 3B
- Flips: 3B

Equipment Needed:
- Exercise tubing
- Sturdy object
- A bat
- Optional: Baseballs, tee
- Batting cage or hitting net

Description: The hitter stands with one end of a piece of exercise tubing looped around his back knee (or attached to a strap on his back knee). The other end of the tubing is secured to a sturdy object like a doorknob or bench, and it is already stretched so it does not fall to the ground. The hitter then swings by pulling the tubing and taking the back knee down to the ground. The hitter needs to work on properly rotating the back foot, finishing on the big toe.

Coaching Points:
- For this drill, the hitter does not stride. He starts wide enough as if he has already taken his stride.
- The hitter should do this drill first with dry swings, and then as he gets better, he can incorporate a tee.
- To give the tubing more resistance, the hitter gets away from the object to which it is secured. To reduce the resistance, the hitter gets closer.

Drill #75: Holding Feet Apart With Tubing

Objectives:
- Improves leg use
- Improves back-foot pivot
- Improves balance

Degree of Difficulty: 3B

Equipment Needed:
- A piece of surgical or exercise tubing
- A bat
- Baseballs
- Partner and batting cage

Description: The hitter first gets a piece of surgical or exercise tubing and does one of the following:
- If the tubing has straps, he can put one inside the back shoe (to force the hitter to pivot the back foot back) and the other strap around the front of the front foot (to keep the front foot closed).

- If his shoes have a small loop by the heel, the hitter can attach the tubing through the loops.
- The hitter can turn both ends into two loops, and then put one inside the back shoe and the other around the front foot.

The tubing has to be stretched enough that it would give the hitter good resistance, but not so tight that he would fall all over the place. The hitter then pivots his back foot by taking the heel back and keeping the feet apart.

Coaching Points:
- The hitter needs to check for cuts and scrapes in the tubing so it does not tear and hurt the hitter.
- The hitter should hold his balance for a count of at least two at the end of the swing.

Drill #76: Extending to Power V With Tubing on the Bat

Objectives:
- Improves arm strength
- Improves core strength
- Improves contact position

Degree of Difficulty: 2B

Equipment Needed:
- Bat
- Tubing
- Partner

Description: The hitter can use an old bat and tape the end of a strip of elastic tubing to the barrel. The other end of the tubing is secured behind him (about waist high) by a strong object. The hitter starts his bat in the bat lag position (bat is parallel to the ground) and then extends to the power V position in which his arms are fully extended, forming a V. The hitter then holds in that position for 5 to 10 seconds or more, depending on the type of condition he is in and the resistance strength of the tubing. To make the drill more difficult, the hitter can point the end of the bat to center field and hold that position.

Coaching Points:
- The hitter does not roll his wrists, but he simply works on stretching the cord only using his hands.
- The hitter needs to check the tubing for cuts and scrapes so the tubing does not snap.

Drill #77: Holding Hands at Different Positions With Tubing on the Bat

Objectives:
- Improves arm strength
- Improves core strength
- Improves contact position

Degree of Difficulty: 2B

Equipment Needed:
- A bat
- Tubing
- Partner

Description: This drill is similar to the previous drill, except the hitter moves his hands to different positions to mimic making contact with pitches at different locations. In every position, the back elbow is in front of the body, but the hands are at different locations. For inside pitches, the hands are on top of the front foot. On pitches in the middle, the hands are right in front of the body but inside the front foot. On outside pitches, the hands are behind the front knee, and the barrel is in an angle back. The hitter can use an old bat and tape the end of a strip of elastic tubing to the barrel. The other end of the tubing is secured behind him (about waist high) by a strong object. The hitter starts his bat in the bat lag position (bat is parallel to the ground) and then extends to the power V position in which his arms are fully extended, forming a V. The hitter then holds in that position for 5 to 10 seconds or more, depending on the type of condition he is in and the resistance strength of the tubing.

Coaching Points:
- The hitter does not roll his wrists, but he simply works on stretching the cord only using his hands.
- The hitter needs to check the tubing for cuts and scrapes so the tubing does not snap.

Drill #78: Tubing From Bicep to Wrist

Objectives:
- Stops casting and improves extension
- Strengthens the hitter's arms

Degree of Difficulty:
- Dry swings: 2B
- Tee work: 2B
- Soft tosses: 2B
- Flips: 2B

Equipment Needed:
- Two straps
- Small tubing
- Tape
- Glasses or goggles

Description: An adult secures the tubing to each one of the straps with enough distance that it would go from the upper arm to the wrist without having so much resistance that the hitter will not be able to extend the arms. The hitter then does a few slow-motion arm extensions with the tubing on the front arm, and then switches the tubing to the back arm. Or, the hitter can work both arms at the same time by placing tubing on both arms. After the hitter gets comfortable and stronger, he can start doing dry swings, then tee work, and so on. For more safety, the hitter should wear glasses or goggles to protect his eyes (just in case).

Coaching Points:
- At the knots, the adult should secure the tubing even more by wrapping the knots with tape.
- Online retailers sell tubing with a sleeve on it for more protection.
- The hitter needs to make sure that the tubing is safe from scratches and cuts.

Drill #79: Tubing From Ground to Waist

Objectives:
- Improves hitting strength
- Improves rotation
- Forces the hitter to stay down

Degree of Difficulty:
- Dry swings: 2B+ (depending on tubing resistance)
- Tee work: 2B

Equipment Needed:
- Piece of board (2 x 48 x 48 inches)
- Two screws with loops/holes, two nuts, four washers
- Belt
- Two pieces of exercise tubing
- Drill

Description: The coach or another adult drills two holes in the board, one at the front end and one at the back end (there should be a straight line between the holes). He sets the screws through the holes. He then secures one end of a piece of exercise tubing to each screw. The other end of each piece of exercise tubing is secured to the belt. The belt is placed around the hitter's waist and the hitter swings, feeling the resistance of the tubing.

Coaching Points:
- Where the tubing is tied to the screws, the coach should secure it even more by wrapping the knots with tape.
- Online retailers sell tubing with a sleeve on it for more protection.
- An alternative to using a board and tubing is to purchase a pre-made device, which can be found in most baseball catalogs.
- The hitter needs to make sure that the tubing is safe from scratches and cuts.

Drill #80: Tubing Resistance at the Waist With a Punching Bag

Objectives:
- Strengthens rotation
- Develops power

Degree of Difficulty:
- Dry swings: 1B
- Tee work: 1B
- Soft tosses: 2B
- Flips: 2B

Equipment Needed:
- A belt
- A piece of surgical or exercise tubing
- Bat and baseballs
- Batting cage
- Pole to tie up tubing

Description: For this drill, the hitter ties the tubing around the belt. He ties the belt around his waist with one end of the tubing on the back hip, and the other end of the tubing tied to a strong pole or something that would not give. Then, the hitter moves forward until the tubing is fully or almost fully stretched, depending on whether or not he strides up and down or steps forward. The hitter sets a punching bag right in front of him. The hitter then swings the bat and hits the punching bag as powerfully as possible, feeling the resistance of the tubing. The hitter can just hit the punching bag and go back to the starting position or he can hold on contact for a count of five, which makes it a lot harder. For more resistance, the hitter should use a stronger cord or stretch the tubing farther. The hitter needs to be strong enough to control the bat from recoiling.

Coaching Point: The hitter needs to make sure that the tubing is safe to use (no cuts or scrapes).

Drill #81: Tubing Resistance on the Bat Barrel With a Punching Bag

Objectives:
- Improves arm strength
- Improves core strength
- Improves contact position

Degree of Difficulty: 3B

Equipment Needed:
- Bat
- Tubing
- Punching bag

Description: The hitter can use an old bat and tape the end of a strip of elastic tubing to the barrel. The other end of the tubing is secured behind him (about waist high) by a strong object. The hitter sets a punching bag right in front of him. The hitter then swings the bat and hits the punching bag as powerfully as possible, feeling the resistance of the tubing. The hitter can just hit the punching bag and go back to the starting position, or he can hold on contact for a count of five, which makes it a lot harder. For more resistance, the hitter should use a stronger cord or stretch the tubing farther. The hitter needs to be strong enough to control the bat from recoiling backwards.

Coaching Points:
- The hitter does not roll his wrists but just work on stretching the cord only using his hands.
- The hitter needs to check the tubing for cuts and scrapes so the tubing does not snap.

8

Drills That Overload the Hitting Muscles Using No Legs

Drill #82: Back Knee on the Ground

Objectives:
- Isolates the upper body
- Teaches the proper use of the hands and arms during the swing
- Isolates the head and increases head control

Degree of Difficulty:
- Dry swings: 1B
- Tee work: 1B
- Soft tosses: 2B
- Flips: 2B

Equipment Needed:
- A bat
- Baseballs
- Batting cage or hitting net
- Optional: Tee, partner, screen

Description: The basic idea of this drill is to work the upper body during the swing. By putting the back knee on the ground, the hitter isolates the upper body, ensuring a better use of his hands and arms, thus teaching his upper body what to do without the bottom half getting in the way. The hitter can position himself for the drill in two ways:
- The hitter puts his back knee on the ground and his front foot flat on the ground with his front knee bent at a 45-degree angle.
- The hitter puts his back knee on the ground, but the front leg is straight, pointing to where the pitcher is in the game, and only the inside of the front foot is on the ground.

After choosing which position is better suited for him, the hitter then takes his swing, finishing it with a follow-through.

Variation: The partner tosses the ball either forehead high or a little higher. The hitter tries to hit a line drive right back to the middle.

Coaching Points:
- The hitter should emphasize throwing his hands to the ball and staying inside the ball.
- He needs to keep his head down throughout the swing for a short and compact swing.
- He needs to pay attention to the entire upper-body hitting mechanics.
- The hitter should do this drill in a carpeted batting cage or on a grassy area to protect his knee. If possible, he should wear a kneepad or catcher's shin guard or put a cushion under his knee.
- If the hitter decides to use the second position, he needs to make sure that he stays inside the ball and hits the ball the other way. If he rolls over or pulls it too much, he could hit the front foot.

Drill #83: Back Knee on the Ground Plus Weight Shift

Objectives:
- Isolates the upper body
- Teaches the proper use of the hands and arms during the swing
- Isolates the head and increases head control

Degree of Difficulty:
- Dry swings: 1B
- Tee work: 1B
- Soft tosses: 2B
- Flips: 2B

Equipment Needed:
- A bat
- Baseballs
- Batting cage or hitting net
- Optional: Tee, partner, screen

Description: This drill adds a weight shift to the previous drill. The hitter puts his back knee on the ground and his front foot flat on the ground with his front knee bent at a 45-degree angle. The hitter then takes his swing and stands up as he finishes the follow-through.

Variation: The partner tosses the ball either forehead high or a little higher. The hitter tries to hit a line drive right back to the middle.

Coaching Points:
- The hitter should emphasize throwing his hands to the ball and staying inside the ball.
- He needs to keep his head down throughout the swing for a short and compact swing.
- He needs to pay attention to the entire upper-body hitting mechanics.
- The hitter should do this drill in a carpeted batting cage or on a grassy area to protect his knee. If possible, he should wear a kneepad or catcher's shin guard or put a cushion under his knee.

Drill #84: Back Foot off the Ground

Objectives:
- Teaches the hitter to swing down
- Improves balance

Degree of Difficulty:
- Dry swings: 1B
- Tee work: 1B
- Soft tosses: 2B
- Flips: 2B

Equipment Needed:
- A bat
- Baseballs
- Batting cage or field
- Partner

Description: This drill will isolate the upper body while helping the hitter learn how to swing right to the ball, thus shortening the swing. To do this drill, the hitter stands with all of his weight on the front leg and with the back foot off the ground. The hitter then goes through his swing process, trying to swing while keeping the back foot from touching the ground. This technique will not only help the hitter use his arms during his swing, but also improve his balance

Coaching Point: This drill will force the hitter to use his hands better. It will also improve balance, especially if the hitter holds at the end of each swing.

Drill #85: Hitting From a Kneeling Position for Proper Arm Use

Objectives:
- Teaches the hitter to use his arms without having the legs involved with the swing
- Teaches the hitter to use his hands and head properly

Degree of Difficulty: 3B

Equipment Needed:
- A bat
- Baseballs
- Batting cage

Description: The hitter gets on his knees. It is like he is at his stance without his legs. The tosser flips the ball to the middle of the plate. The hitter tries to hit the ball right back to the tosser, who is hiding behind a screen. The hitter needs to work on swinging the bat by having his chin going front shoulder to back shoulder or at least by finishing the swing with the chin on the back shoulder.

Coaching Point: The hitter should do this drill in a carpeted batting cage or on a grassy area to protect his knees. If possible, he should wear kneepads or catcher's shin guards or put cushions under his knees.

Drill #86: Hitting Without a Stride

Objectives:
- Teaches proper use of the hands
- Improves your hitting mechanics
- Teaches you to hit the inside of the ball and hitting to the opposite field
- Provides upper body hitting practice

Degree of Difficulty:
- Dry swings: 1B
- Tee work: 1B
- Soft tosses: 2B
- Flips: 2B
- Batting practice: 3B

Equipment Needed:
- A bat
- Baseballs
- Batting cage, net, or field
- Optional: Tee

Description: Two variations of this drill are as follows:
- The hitter sets his feet apart as if he has already taken his stride. He waits for the ball to get to him, without moving his front foot. He then takes his swing, using only his upper body while keeping the back foot planted on the ground all the way through the swing (he does not pivot).
- The hitter puts his front foot as if he has already taken his stride. He waits for the ball to get to him, without moving his front foot. Then, he takes his regular swing, emphasizing what the upper body is doing and the proper pivot of the back foot. The hitter needs to wait a little longer on the ball and stay inside of the ball.

Coaching Points:
- The hitter can do this drill on his first round of batting practice, to hit the ball the other way and to get the feeling of waiting back.
- The hitter needs to work on staying inside the ball and hitting the ball the opposite way.
- As with any drill, the hitter should do 10-plus-5 routines so he keeps the feeling of the drill during his regular swings.

Drill #87: Hitting From a Stool

Objectives:
- Teaches the hitter to properly use his upper body
- Teaches the hitter to use his hands and arms during the swing
- Teaches the hitter to hit through the ball

Degree of Difficulty:
- Dry swings: 2B
- Tee work: 2B
- Soft tosses: 3B
- Flips: 3B

Equipment Needed:
- Stool, chair, or bench
- A bat
- Baseballs
- Tee
- Partner

Description: The hitter sits on a stool. He swings the bat, paying attention to all the components of his upper-body swing:
- Hitting box
- Taking the hands back
- Swing path
- Contact
- Follow-through

By sitting on the stool, the hitter will be able to isolate the upper body, allowing him to learn how to use that part of his swing. With the hitter not worrying about using his legs, and the legs not getting in the way of the swing, the hitter will be able to practice the proper mechanics of the arms and the head during the swing.

Coaching Points:
- The hitter needs to get the back elbow in front of the chest and keep his head down on contact.
- A good hitting box has the elbows pointing down to the ground, and the hands on top of the hitter's strike zone.
- The hitter should start this drill by doing dry swings. He can then move to the tee or even do soft tosses.
- Batting practice is not recommended for this drill.
- The hitter needs to hit through the ball. He needs to push the ball away from him by having the bat follow the ball for as long as possible.

Drill #88: Hitting From an Exercise Ball

Objectives:
- Teaches the hitter to properly use his upper body
- Teaches the hitter to use his hands and arms during the swing
- Strengthens the hitters mid section
- Teaches the hitter to hit through the ball

Degree of Difficulty:
- Dry swings: 2B
- Tee work: 2B
- Soft tosses: 3B
- Flips: 3B

Equipment Needed:
- Exercise ball (Swiss ball)
- A bat
- Baseballs
- Tee
- Partner

Description: The hitter sits on an exercise ball. He swings the bat, paying attention to all the components of his upper-body swing:
- Hitting box
- Taking the hands back
- Swing path
- Contact
- Follow-through

By sitting on the exercise ball, the hitter will be able to isolate the upper body, allowing him to learn how to use it better. With the hitter not worrying about using his legs, and the legs not getting in the way of the swing, the hitter will be able to practice the proper mechanics of the arms and the head during the swing. This drill is better than the hitting from a stool drill because it improves the hitter's balance and the strength of his core area, and because the ball rolls underneath the hitter, it gives him feedback when he is drifting.

Coaching Points:
- The hitter needs to get the back elbow in front of the chest and keep his head down on contact.
- A good hitting box has the elbows pointing down to the ground and the hands on top of the hitter's strike zone.
- The hitter should start this drill by doing dry swings. He can then move to the tee or even do soft tosses.
- Batting practice is not recommended for this drill.
- The hitter needs to hit through the ball. He needs to push the ball away from him by having the bat follow the ball for as long as possible.

Drill #89: Ankle Weights to Keep Feet in Place

Objectives:
- Improves the use of the hands
- Quiets happy feet to concentrate the hitter in one spot to generate maximum power without wasting in motion during the swing

Degree of Difficulty:
- Dry swings: 1B
- Tee work: 1B
- Soft tosses: 2B
- Flips: 2B
- Batting practice/machine: 3B

Equipment Needed:
- Two ankle weights (the heavier, the better)
- A bat
- Baseballs
- Optional: Partner, tee

Description: For this drill, the hitter needs two ankle weights (the heavier, the better). He ties the weights around his ankles and tries to swing the bat as he normally does. The weight will force him to keep the feet in place, giving him instant feedback on how and where he is moving his feet. This drill is helpful for hitters who have happy feet (moving feet too much) and to show the hitter how to stay in place during the swing.

Coaching Points:
- After the hitter gets used to using his arms properly, he can incorporate a back-foot pivot.
- The weight will give the hitter instant feedback as to how and where the hitter is moving his feet.

9

Drills That Overload the Hitting Muscles Using Different Exercises

Drill #90: Medicine Ball Tosses

Objectives:
- Strengthens the core area
- Improves explosiveness and power
- Improves midsection range of motion
- Improves muscular endurance

Degree of Difficulty: 1B

Equipment Needed:
- Medicine ball
- Concrete wall
- Partner

Description: Using the medicine ball targets the core area (abs, lower back, hips, buttocks, and thighs), which is the center of power and balance. Focusing on the core area is a must if a hitter wants to develop explosive hitting power. These exercises help apply and transfer the strength gained in the weight room to the hitter's swing more specifically. The following exercises should be performed:

- Swing toss to the wall (Figures A and B)
- Swing toss over front leg (Figures C and D)
- Short toss (Figures E and F)
- Side to side (Figures G through I)

The hitter should do sets of three to six reps if he is working on explosion and sets of 10 reps if he is working on muscular endurance.

Coaching Points:
- The exercises should be done in a controlled manner. The hitter needs to accelerate and decelerate in control, even though these exercises are done explosively.
- These exercises should be done with a lot of intensity (moderate to fast speed).
- Younger hitters can use a basketball or a similarly sized ball.
- The hitter should get used to the exercise before increasing the speed.

Figure A

Figure B

Figure C

Figure D

Figure E

Figure F

Figure G

Figure H

Figure I

125

Drill #91: Cable and Medicine Ball Swings

Objectives:
- Strengthens the hitting muscles
- Mimics the swing action

Degree of Difficulty: 2B

Equipment Needed:
- Tubing
- Medicine ball
- Cable machine

Description:
❑ Swing Down
- Medicine ball (Figures A and B): The hitter holds the ball over and away from the head (starts with the side he regularly hits), and then diagonally takes the medicine ball to the outside opposite knee or hip (trying to keep the ball within the chin and the belly button).
- Tubing: The hitter sets one handle to something higher than his head (sturdy and strong). With both hands, he grabs the tubing's other handle. He starts with the hands close to his launching position (or higher), and then takes the handle (stretching the tubing) to the opposite side hip or knee.

Figure A

Figure B

Figure C

Figure D

- Cable machine (Figures C and D): The hitter attaches the single-arm handle to the cable attachment. The hitter then sets the handle to the top of the machine to about where his hands are at the launching position. The hitter holds the handle like he does his normal bat. He then brings the handle down, mimicking his swing.
❏ Swing Up
- Medicine ball (Figures E and F): The hitter holds the ball outside his knee or hip, and then diagonally takes the medicine ball to the opposite ear (over and away from the head).
- Tubing (Figures G and H): The hitter sets one handle to something low (floor or knee level). With both hands, he grabs the tubing's other handle. He starts with the hands outside one of the hips or knee. He then takes the handle (stretching the tubing) to the opposite side of the head.
- Cable machine: The hitter sets the attachment at the bottom of the machine. The hitter then brings both arms together, with the hands all the way up to or over the head. The hitter does not need to do this drill explosively; instead, he needs to develop strength at the rotation muscles.

Coaching Points:
- If possible, the hitter should swing his bat after performing the drill.
- The hitter needs to concentrate on strength by doing slow, coordinated reps.

Figure E

Figure F

Figure G

Figure H

Drill #92: Rotation Exercises for Hitting Power

Objectives:
- Improves strength in the midsection
- Helps stabilize the trunk area
- Improves endurance in the midsection
- Improves coordination
- Improves midsection functionality and rotational power
- Improves performance
- Helps prevent injuries of the midsection, especially of the lower back

Degree of Difficulty: 2B

Equipment Needed:
- Medicine ball
- Chair
- Open area

Description: To hit the ball hard, the hitter needs to have a strong midsection. Most of the hitting power is developed in this area. For a hitter, this part of the training program is the most important. The core is the center of the body, and all movements originate there. The core includes the abdominal muscles (lower, upper, and obliques), lower back, buttocks,

Figure A

Figure B

Figure C

Figure D

Figure E

Figure F

Figure G

hips, and thighs. Hitting requires acceleration, deceleration, and stabilization of the core area. The exercises are as follows:

- Medicine ball over head trunk twist with wall touch (Figure A)
- Medicine ball half-trunk twist (Figure B)
- Medicine ball full-trunk twist (Figure C)
- Seated medicine ball trunk twist toss to partner (Figures D through G)
- Trunk twist wall touch (Figure H)
- Regular trunk twist (Figure I)
- Chair trunk twist (Figure J)
- Medicine ball standing trunk twist with pause in the middle (Figure K)
- Seated medicine ball trunk twist with floor touch (Figure L)

Coaching Points:

- The hitter can pick two or three of these exercises and do two or three sets of about 10 repetitions every other day.
- The hitter should use proper form and keep proper posture when doing the exercises. He should concentrate on quality not quantity.
- The hitter should do the exercises slowly and in a controlled manner.
- The hitter can protect the spine from injury by doing controlled movements and keeping the spine in a neutral pain-free position during the exercises.

Figure H

Figure I

Figure J

Figure K

Figure L

Drill #93: Medicine Ball Slam

Objectives:
- Improves strength in the midsection
- Helps stabilize the trunk area
- Improves endurance in the midsection
- Improves coordination
- Improves midsection functionality and rotational power
- Improves performance
- Helps prevent injuries of the midsection, especially of the lower back

Degree of Difficulty: 2B

Equipment Needed: Medicine ball with a rope through it (tornado ball, etc.) or a towel and medicine ball or basketball (depending on hitter's age, strength, and skill)

Description: To hit the ball hard, the hitter needs to have a strong midsection. Most of the hitting power is developed in this area. For a hitter, this part of the training program is the most important. The core is the center of the body, and all movements originate there. The core includes the abdominal muscles (lower, upper, and obliques), lower back, buttocks, hips, and thighs. Hitting requires acceleration, deceleration, and stabilization of the core area. To do this drill the hitter can use two types of equipment:
- A medicine ball that comes with a rope through the poles of the ball.
- A medicine ball sling, which holds different size medicine balls, or a medicine ball with a towel wrapped around it (if he wants, he can tape a handle for a better grip).

The exercises are as follows:
- Two-hand side-to-side wall slam (Figure A)
- Diagonal (woodchops) wall slam (Figure B)
- Swing wall slam (Figures C and D)
- Swing toss (Figures E and F)
- One-arm side-to-side wall slam (Figure G)

Coaching Points:
- The hitter should use proper form and keep proper posture when doing the exercises. He should concentrate on quality not quantity.
- The hitter should stop if his back hurts or starts to arch.
- When doing rotation work, the hitter should start slow, keeping proper lower-back posture.
- The hitter should find a position in which he is still comfortable and pain-free when the spine muscles are being tightened during the exercise. He should protect the spine from injury by doing controlled movements, keeping the spine in a neutral, pain-free position during the exercises. For the beginning position:
  ✓ The knees are flexed.
  ✓ The abs are tightened.
  ✓ The spine muscles are tightened.

Figure A

Figure B

Figure C

Figure D

Figure E

Figure F

Figure G

Drill #94: Swing Pulldown

Objectives:
- Develops power (overload)
- Develops bat speed (overspeed)
- Simulates swing
- Develops explosiveness
- Increases muscle strength for hitting

Degree of Difficulty: 2B

Equipment Needed:
- Pulldown machine (at a gym)
- Rope triceps grip
- Optional: Weight, rope, and pulley
- Optional: A bat
- Optional: Baseballs

Description: The hitter attaches the rope grip used for doing triceps extensions to a pulldown machine. He holds one side of the rope as if he were holding his bat (he needs to experiment with the weight—not too heavy and not too light). He proceeds to mimic his swing all the way to his follow-through. As he gets stronger, the hitter needs to increase the weight. For better results with this drill, the hitter can execute a few swings with his bat, if an open space is available

(Note: He should only do so if other people are not around). This program will overload the hitter's hitting muscles and overspeed his swing, helping him develop more power and bat speed.

A swing pulldown can be made using a pulley (available from a hardware store for a couple of dollars). The pulley can be attached to a tree, the top of a batting cage, or a similar structure and a 25-pound plate can be tied at one end while the other end is used as a bat grip. It is pretty easy and inexpensive to make if the weight is available.

Coaching Points:
- The hitter should wear batting gloves to avoid blisters.
- The hitter should complete as many reps as he can do in a row.
- This drill should be done two to three times a week, and never before a game.
- If the hitter does not lift weight, he can use exercise tubing, which is sold in sporting goods stores and comes in different levels of resistance. This tubing can offer good resistance, and could serve as transition to prepare the hitter for weight training.

Drill #95: Barbell Rotational Exercises

Objective: Improves strength

Degree of Difficulty: 3B

Equipment Needed:
- Barbell
- Dumbbell

Description: The hitter needs to make sure that he uses a weight that he can handle. The exercises are as follows:

- Barbell trunk twist (Figure A): The hitter places a barbell on the shoulders and turns from side to side.
  - ✓ This exercise can be done without stopping, keeping good rhythm.
  - ✓ The exercise can also be done by stopping at the halfway point, and then going back to the same side or going to the other side.
  - ✓ This exercise can be done at a fast pace.
- Lunge and twist (Figure B): The hitter lunges forward and turns toward the leg that is lunging.

Figure A

Figure B

Drill #96: Explosive Rotational Exercises

Objectives:
- Helps the hitter hit the ball harder
- Helps the hitter develop more bat speed

Degree of Difficulty: 3B

Equipment Needed:
- Barbell
- Dumbbell

Description: The game of baseball—and hitting especially—requires explosive movements. It requires the hitter to develop the greatest amount of force in the shortest amount of time. To do so, the hitter needs to be both strong and fast. The following exercises require explosive moves to be performed and will help the hitter develop more power:
- Barbell side twist (Figures A and B)
- Twist with two hands in front of the body (Figure C)
- Squat and turn (Figures D and E)

Coaching Points:
- The hitter should use controlled movements.
- The essence of power is speed, so the hitter should avoid using too heavy of a resistance, which will slow him down. Instead, he should use a moderate weight and do the exercises as explosively as possible, keeping balance and control throughout.
- The hitter should practice the exercises with a lot of intensity.

Figure A

Figure B

Figure C

Figure D

Figure E

Drill #97: Stick-With-Weight Arm Swings

Objective: Strengthens the forearms and wrists to swing more powerfully

Degree of Difficulty: 2B

Equipment Needed:
- Weight plate (1, 2 1/2, and/or 5 pounds)
- Broken wood bat handle or dowel
- Washer
- Nail

Description: This drill will overload the hitting muscles and help the hitter hit the ball harder. To create the weighted stick for this drill, the hitter should attach a weight to the end of a bat handle or dowel using a washer and nail. The hitter performs his regular swing with the weighted stick. He should also do one-arm swings simply by extending the elbow. He can also strengthen his wrists and forearms by doing the following exercises:

Figure A

Figure B

- Up and down (Figure A)
- Supination (Figure B)
- Pronation (Figure C)
- Ulnar deviation (Figure D)
- Rotational wrist exercises: The hitter moves the weight in a circle, keeping the forearm on the leg.

Coaching Points:
- The hitter needs to make sure to warm up before he does any of these exercises.
- A good program would be doing a couple of sets of 10 repetitions of each exercise.

- The hitter has the option to swing the bat if he desires after doing these exercises.
- Stronger hands and forearms are important for solid contact because the fingers hold the bat, so the hitter needs to keep the forearms strong.
- The hitter should always use a weight that he can control, and squeeze when doing the movement.
- The hitter should grip the stick as if he were gripping a bat with the thumb around the rest of the fingers. This technique will make his grip stronger.

Figure C

Figure D

Drill #98: Forearm Workout

Objective: Strengthens forearms, fingers, hands, and wrists

Degree of Difficulty: 2B+

Equipment Needed:
- Bat(s)
- Rice and bucket
- PVC pipe
- Hand grippers, or rubber ball cut in half, or tennis ball
- Rope, pipe or dowel, and weight plate or dumbbell

Description: The following exercises are done to strengthen the forearms, wrists, hands, and fingers:
- Wrist curls (Figures A and B): With a barbell on his hands and the forearms resting on the thighs (hands outside the knees), the hitter rolls the barbell through his fingers and then rolls it back up to a fist.
- Hammer curls with hold (Figure C): The hitter curls the weight until the forearms are parallel to the ground. The hitter then holds the weight for as long as possible.
- Grip strength drill (Figure D): The hitter uses hand grippers, which can be bought at any sporting goods or department store, or a rubber ball cut in half (a half for each hand) or tennis balls. The hitter does sets of 10 repetitions with each hand. To make the hand-grip workout more challenging, the hitter can try to squeeze a coin for as long as possible.

- Squeeze a tennis ball (Figure E): Done like the grip strength drill, but using a tennis ball or a rubber ball cut in half.
- Holding weighted plate (Figure F): The hitter holds different-sized weight plates with his fingers for as long as possible.
- Power V: A partner stands in front of the hitter with a bat (PVC pipe, regular bat, or heavy bat) at about the hitter's waist and parallel to the ground. The hitter stands with the elbows close to the body and with the bat or pipe below the partner's bat. The hitter proceeds to mimic a V, having the bat going to the left and to the right of the partner's object without moving the arms, simply using the wrists.
- Rice in the bucket: A bucket is filled with rice. The hitter then squeezes the rice, turning the hands outward and holding the rice for a count.
- Wrist roller: The hitter can tie one end of a rope to a pipe or dowel and the other end to a weight plate or dumbbell (less than 10 pounds). He rolls the rope around the pipe or dowel until the weight is almost touching the pipe. He then unrolls the rope, slowly lowering the weight to the starting position.

Coaching Points:
- The hitter can do reps of five per direction and per arm.
- The hitter can alternate with slow-motion movements to get the muscles stronger and faster movements to burn and condition them.
- The hitter needs to make sure to warm up properly before doing these exercises.

Figure A

Figure B

Figure C

Figure D

Figure E

Figure F

Drill #99: Torso Rotation With Tubing

Objectives:
- Improves strength in the torso area
- Improves rotation (keeps hitter in same location throughout the swing)

Degree of Difficulty: 2B

Equipment Needed:
- Exercise tubing
- Pole or doorknob
- Optional: A bat

Description: The hitter secures one end of the exercise tubing to a pipe, doorknob, or any other similar object at about navel height. Then, holding the other end of the tubing with both hands, the hitter does a set of torso rotations to strengthen his midsection and to improve his rotation during the swing. The exercises are as follows:
- Turn and extend (Figures A and B): The hitter holds one of the handles with both hands. He turns as if he is doing a swing. After the tubing has gone in front of his body, he lets go of the bottom hand and keeps stretching the tubing until the top arm is fully extended.
- Inward rotation (Figures C and D): The hitter holds each handle with each hand. He then brings both handles to his side, trying to take the handle past the body.

Coaching Points:
- To increase resistance, the hitter can stretch the cord or double it up.
- For his protection, the hitter needs to make sure to check the tubing for cracks before using it.
- After each set of the drill, the hitter can swing his regular bat.
- Check the tubing before using (holes, tears, overuse).
- The hitter should warm up before performing these exercises.
- The more the hitter stretches the cord or the more he wraps the ends around his hands, the more resistance it provides.
- Exercise tubing comes in different resistance levels. The hitter should find the level that makes him work with intensity.
- The hitter should never pull the tubing toward his face or others around him.
- The hitter should use a strong object (such as a door or a squat rack) to secure the tubing.
- The hitter should start with one or two sets of 8 to 10 reps per exercise, three days a week, with a day in between. He can move up, depending on his training goals.

Figure A

Figure B

Figure C

Figure D

Drill #100: Abs Training

Objective: Strengthens the abdominal muscles

Degree of Difficulty: 2B

Equipment Needed: None

Description: The abs are a big part of the core area (midsection) of the body where most of the rotational power of the swing is developed. The abs muscles are divided into four sections: upper, middle, lower, and side or obliques. All of them are important for the hitter, but a lot of emphasis should be put on developing the side abs muscles because of the rotation of the swing. The tempo of each exercise should be slow and controlled, holding for a count of two in between. This holding will help the hitter target the whole set of abs muscles instead of just the muscle usually isolated by that particular exercise. The hitter should keep the reps between 10 and 15 and the sets to one or two of each exercise. The following exercises should be performed:

- Sit-up with feet raises (Figures A and B)
- Swiss knife (Figures C and D)
- Core control (Figure E)
- Bicycle (Figure F)
- Sit-up and hold for set time (Figure G)
- Heel touches (Figure H)

Coaching Points:
- The hitter does not need to do hundreds of repetitions to get his abs stronger and more defined. The abs muscle tissue is the same as that of the chest and the biceps, so it is better to do fewer reps with some resistance than hundreds of reps without it. The idea is to get stronger, and the only way the hitter will develop more strength is by overloading the muscles.
- The hitter can add resistance to the exercises but should not use too much resistance. Excessive resistance does not allow the hitter to do the exercise properly and increases the chances of injury. It is better to use less resistance and better form rather than a lot of resistance and improper form. To add resistance, the hitter can use one of the following:
  ✓ Free weights (plates, dumbbells)
  ✓ Medicine balls
  ✓ Inclining the angle of the sit-up bench
  ✓ Cable machine with ankle attachments
  ✓ Abs machines
  ✓ Ankle weights
- The hitter should make sure that his back is flat on the surface (floor, bench) used, to avoid lower-back problems.
- The hitter should make sure to keep muscle balance by doing lower-back exercises either before or after the abs workout.

Figure A

Figure B

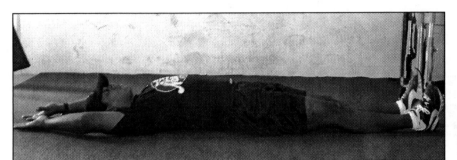

Figure C

Figure D

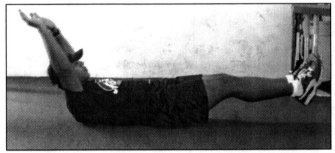

Figure E

Figure F

Figure G

Figure H

Drill #101: Core Training

Objectives:
- Improves balance in the midsection (trunk and pelvis muscles)
- Improves strength in the midsection
- Helps stabilize the trunk area
- Improves endurance in the midsection
- Improves coordination
- Improves midsection functionality and rotational power
- Improves performance
- Helps prevent injuries of the midsection especially of the lower back

Degree of Difficulty: 2B

Equipment Needed: Stability ball

Description: To hit the ball hard, the hitter needs to have a strong midsection. Most of the hitting power is developed in this area. For a hitter, this part of the training program is the most important. The core is the center of the body, and all movements originate there. The core includes the abdominal muscles (lower, upper, and obliques), lower back, buttocks, hips, and thighs. Hitting requires acceleration,

Figure A

Figure B

Figure C

Figure D

Figure E

deceleration, and stabilization of the core area. The following exercises should be performed slowly and in a controlled manner:

- Superman (Figure A)
- Quadruple—switching hands and legs (Figure B)
- Cobra (Figures C and D)
- Alternating Superman (Figure E)
- Leg raises on exercise ball (Figures F and G)
- Dead bug—alternating arms and legs (Figure H)
- Planks—holding for 30 to 60 seconds (Figure I)
- Plank with leg switch (Figure J)
- Side plank—holding for 20 to 60 seconds (Figure K)
- Reverse plank—holding for 30 to 60 seconds (Figure L)
- Extended-arm plank—holding for 10 seconds or more (Figure M)

Coaching Points:

- The hitter should use proper form and keep proper posture when doing the exercises. He should concentrate on quality not quantity.
- The hitter should keep the spine in a neutral, pain-free position during the exercises.
- As the hitter gets stronger, he can add reps and weights (light ankle/wrist weights), regular weights, and balls.

Figure F

Figure G

Figure H

Figure I

Figure J

Figure K

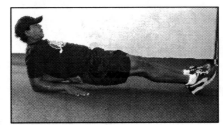

Figure L

Figure M

About the Author

Luis Ortiz is the hitting coordinator for the Texas Rangers. Previously, he played at both the Minor and Major League levels. His time in the Major League included stints with the Red Sox and the Texas Rangers. For most of his Minor League career, he maintained a batting average over .300.

After growing up playing baseball in the Dominican Republic, Luis earned a baseball scholarship from Union University in Jackson, TN, where he set many of Union's batting average and home run records, as well as the NAIA career slugging percentage record. In 1991, Luis was drafted in the eighth round by the Boston Red Sox. While still playing, Luis went back to school 13 years after his first college stint and graduated with a bachelor's degree in physical education. Luis has been offered numerous coaching positions with professional organizations.

His books *The Natural Hitter's Handbook, The Natural Hitter's Drill Handbook Vol. 1: 101 Basic Hitting Drills*, and *Vol. 2: 101 Advanced Hitting Drills* are also available from Coaches Choice, along with the following videos:

- *50 Things a Hitter Needs to Do to Be Successful at the Plate*
- *Effective Practice Drills for Throwing a Baseball*
- *Getting Yourself in Position to Hit the Ball Harder*
- *How to Throw a Baseball Like a Pro*
- *Improving Your Swing Path to Hit the Ball Harder*
- *Natural Hitter's Drills: Vol. 1— Developing Hitting Strength*
- *Natural Hitter's Drills: Vol. 2—Developing Bat Speed*

Information about lessons and video analysis is available at www.ortizbaseball.com.